CRIES OF THE WILD

A WILDLIFE REHABILITATOR'S JOURNAL

JEFF LEDERMAN

Foreword by Malcolm McAdie
Illustrations by Donald Gunn
Environmental Essays by Stefania Gaspari

Heritage House Publishing Company Ltd.

CANADIAN CATALOGUING IN PUBLICATION DATA
Lederman, Jeff
Cries of the Wild

ISBN 1-895811-46-5

1. Lederman, Jeff
2. Wildlife Rehabilitation, Saltspring Island
3. Island Wildlife Natural Care Centre
I. Title

SF996.36.L42A3 1997 639.96092 C97-910624-9

First Edition 1997

Heritage House wishes to acknowledge the support of Heritage Canada,
the British Columbia Arts Council, the Cultural Services Branch of the
Ministry of Small Business, Tourism and Culture, and BC Parks.

Cover, Book Design & Typesetting by Catherine Mack, Cairn Consulting
Edited by Edna Sheedy and Audrey McClellan

HERITAGE HOUSE PUBLISHING COMPANY LTD.
Unit #8 - 17921 55th Ave., Surrey, BC V3S 6C4

Printed in Canada on Recycled Paper

CONTENTS

FOREWORD

In the fifteenth century, when Spanish explorers first arrived on the shores of the North American continent, there existed a natural abundance and diversity that we can only imagine and marvel at today. Extensive, undisturbed hardwood forests covered much of the eastern continent and ancient temperate rain forests cloaked the Pacific Northwest. Life on the great plains was dominated by a vast herd of bison that may have contained up to sixty million animals. California condors patrolled the skies from British Columbia to Baja California, and the passenger pigeon formed flocks so extensive that they blotted out the sun.

Today, the eastern forests have been virtually eliminated by logging and urban development, and the remaining stands of temperate rain forest are being decimated at an alarming rate. The great bison herd has been reduced to a few scattered remnants, the California condor survives only as a result of intensive captive management, and the passenger pigeon is a faded memory, preserved in the form of a few historical accounts and mounted specimens. It is only now, when we are on the verge of losing much of our wilderness and wildlife, that we have come to realize how truly special and valuable it is.

It is almost impossible to comprehend the extent to which we have altered our world. Extensive roads and metropolitan areas fragment and isolate our remaining wild areas. Our air and water have become seriously polluted as a result of the by-products of industry and agriculture. Our insatiable need for electricity has created a lethal network of power lines which causes an untold number of wildlife injuries and fatalities each year. In addition to dealing with the age-old natural struggle of procuring food, defending a territory, and reproducing, modern wildlife must now cope with a wide array of human-made obstacles and threats.

Understaffed and underfunded wildlife agencies are given the overwhelming task of preserving wildlife populations and habitat against this onslaught of human influence. Unfortunately, these agencies often lack the necessary resources or mandate to deal effectively with the individual wild animals that are so often affected by our many activities.

What would be the fate of a raccoon that has been hit by a car, an eagle that is convulsing from the effects of a pesticide, or a heron that is suffering from burns as a result of an electrocution were it not for the efforts of dedicated wildlife rehabilitators such as Jeff Lederman? These individuals have dedicated their resources, their energies, and their lives towards the care of orphaned, ill, and injured wildlife. Through their work, wildlife rehabilitators demonstrate that the individual wild animal is indeed important, and that it is worthy of our humane consideration and respect. We owe Jeff and his colleagues tremendous gratitude for confronting a multitude of problems that we have all helped create.

I have often wondered what motivates wildlife rehabilitators to persevere in such a demanding field. They may have to decide to end a wild animal's suffering when its injuries are too severe or painful for it to live. Or they may have an animal die in their hands after their best efforts have failed.

Maybe it is the successes, and not the failures, that allow wildlife rehabilitators to continue against heavy financial, physical, and emotional odds. They can experience the joy that comes from restoring an injured eagle to full health or from raising an orphaned seal pup to the point of self-sufficiency. Perhaps the greatest motivation for wildlife rehabilitators comes at the time of a successful release, when the eagle rises on the thermals or the seal pup swims gracefully through its aquatic world. At that time there is a sense of liberation and kinship that most people will never know in the insulated, mechanized world that they have created for themselves.

By experiencing the life of a wildlife rehabilitator through the stories of Jeff Lederman, the reader will gain a greater insight into and empathy for our natural world and its inhabitants. It is my hope that the reader will also gain a heightened appreciation for the plight of our wildlife and be motivated to help. Just as each wild animal is important, so is the contribution that each of us can make in working to conserve our wild resources. Do we need to lose our remaining wilderness and wildlife in order to realize how truly special and valuable it is?

Malcolm McAdie, Doctor of Veterinary Medicine
B.C. Ministry of Environment

INTRODUCTION

If you had told me ten years ago what I would be doing today, I would have said you were crazy. I spent most of my life as an artist. I lived and worked in lofts and abandoned factories resurrected by urban artists, in neighborhoods that were the backdrop for society's nightmares.

Living in an intense urban environment, one has a tendency to become so fixated on the day-to-day struggle to survive, pay your bills, and avoid being victimized that it is difficult to comprehend what is going on outside the city. For me, at least, this was a selfish, self-involved lifestyle. Yet in so many ways it was the fulfillment of my fantasies.

The thing about fantasies, though, is that you can't dream of things when you have no awareness of their existence. You can sense a longing for something different without knowing what you long for. Or you may be aware of an inexplicable emptiness in your life. Such was the case with my life.

As a city dweller I had absolutely no knowledge of the natural world— and no concern about it, for that matter. Loss of habitat meant I had to find a new apartment. A wildlife corridor was the alley behind my building where the rats ran. And a fecal examination was checking the bottoms of my shoes to see what I had stepped in. News of clear-cutting, species extinction, water pollution, and the myriad other environmental crises fell on deaf ears. I ate at McDonalds, I never bought animal-safe products, I owned a fur coat!

Although what transpired was a slow progression, it seemed that one morning I awoke in northern New Mexico, in the body of a wildlife rehabilitator. Now this is what I mean when I say you can't dream of things that you don't know exist. What in the world is a wildlife rehabilitator? I had never heard of such a thing. Of course I had heard of zoos, aquariums, and veterinary clinics, but a wildlife rehabilitation centre? Never.

I had been living in the New Mexico countryside, making art, when my friend Lill told me of a raptor rehabilitation facility about ten minutes from my house. I visited and I was hooked. I don't know why. Until that time I'd had only a very casual interest in animals, mostly birds. The workers at the rehab facility took me inside a large flight cage with half a dozen golden eagles. The eagles flew over us and we had to duck so the wings wouldn't hit us. I never thought I could be so close to so many incredible birds of prey. It didn't seem like a life-altering experience, but I found myself volunteering 40 hours a week, and that's about all I've done since. I guess the time was just right.

Today I am dedicated to relieving the pain and suffering of the wild animals in the area where I live, whether that is New Mexico, California, or the islands along the Canada-U.S. boundary in the Strait of Georgia. In recent years I have worked my way north up the west coast from California to Washington and British Columbia—a glorious natural environment embraced by virtually everyone who discovers it. In 1997 I founded the Island Wildlife Natural Care Centre, a wildlife rehabilitation centre on Saltspring Island, B.C. It is equipped to care for all indigenous wildlife of the Gulf Islands, from birds to marine mammals.

The centre specializes in alternative treatments such as homeopathy, herbal remedies, and physical therapies. These days, the environment and especially the oceans have become so toxic that I feel it is of the utmost importance not to add to the animals' chemical load. A healthy immune system is paramount to survival. There is a great deal of evidence that allopathic (conventional) drug use compromises various organs and suppresses immune response. Properly prescribed homeopathic and herbal remedies can stimulate and support the animals' natural defenses. Homeopathy and carefully applied herbal remedies have no side effects or harmful interactions.

More than 90 percent of the animals admitted to wildlife centres are there because of an unfortunate interaction with humans. For centuries, humanity has waged an ill-conceived assault on the natural world and survival for most wild animals is precarious at best. As you will read in these stories, innocent animals are constantly slammed by automobiles, poisoned by industrial, agricultural, and household chemicals, trapped in machinery and construction sites, shot by people who don't value life, drowned in fishing gear...

I am frequently told that wildlife rehabilitation has no real importance and no impact on species populations as a whole. While this may be true, the work I do means everything to a fawn who has just been made an orphan by an automobile, to a harbour seal pup dying slowly on a beach because its mother drowned in a fishing net, or to a bald eagle electrocuted on a power line. I see animals as independent lives, not as populations. If I can prevent the needless suffering of a single animal, then I have done important work.

The stories collected here were never intended to be a book. They are my vivid memories of some of the animals that I have had the great privilege to be close to. The images that accompany the stories are, for the most part, snapshots and video images that I accumulated as a matter of record, never intending them for publication. There is something very personal about this wildlife work. On one level, sharing these stories and images with the world feels a bit like an invasion of my privacy.

However, on another level, and perhaps much more important than my personal feelings, I hope these stories and images will inspire readers to tread more softly on the earth, help an injured animal find its way to a rehabilitation centre, drive a little more slowly in areas inhabited by animals, and become aware that every action you take has some impact on life somewhere else. The insects you poison around the house will in turn poison the birds and lizards that feed on them. The drain cleaners and outdated prescriptions you pour into a sink or toilet will find their way to the rivers, lakes, and oceans. The minutes you save by hurrying in your car may cost the lives of a doe and her dependent fawn.

I hope these stories bring you a little of the joy, heartbreak, and inspiration that these incredible animals have brought to me. As you read about the struggles and triumphs, keep in mind that this is costly work. X rays, blood tests, medications, specialized diets, safe housing, and thousands of pounds of herring all add up to a significant annual budget. Island Wildlife Natural Care Centre is a registered charity staffed completely by volunteers. Your donations are the means by which we can continue this life-saving work.

Jeff Lederman
Island Wildlife Natural Care Centre
322 Langs Road, Saltspring Island
British Columbia   V8K 1N3 Canada

LUMINA & THE KILLER WHALE

Harbour Seal pupping season is both demanding and intense. We can easily receive up to sixty orphaned pups over a three-month period. The rescues themselves are often as exciting as the triumph of rehabilitation, and every individual case lives in my memory.

The Harbour Seal, able to dive as deep as ninety meters, remain underwater for up to twenty minutes, and travel up rivers for miles in pursuit of food, is a fascinating mammal. And if there's anything cuter than a Harbour Seal pup, I've yet to see it.

When the telephone rings and someone reports a Seal pup in trouble, the rescue might be as routine as a walk down a beach to pick up an exhausted and emaciated animal. It could mean I have to rappel down a small cliff to snatch an unconscious pup off the rocks before the tide takes it out to sea and drowns it. Or it could be a story like Lumina's.

My good friend Joe Luma owns a Bed and Breakfast close to the Wildlife Centre. Late one afternoon Joe came by to report that two of his guests, on an early–morning kayaking expedition, had discovered a Seal pup on a small island beach. It was alone and crying continuously. Because it's not uncommon for mother Seals to leave their pups on the beach for a short while, this pup was not necessarily in any danger. But I have learned never to assume the best, and Joe apparently shared my perspective. His truck was already in the parking lot, hitched to a trailer that held his two-person sea kayak. He was way ahead of me.

It was late in the day, and the overcast sky drizzled rain as we slid the kayak into the water. We paddled hard for about thirty minutes to reach the island, not wanting to waste any time. There would be little chance of spotting the pup after sundown.

Joe had mounted special clips on his kayak to hold the large aluminum net I always bring along on sea rescues. I also carry an electrolyte solution and stomach tube, so I can immediately begin rehydrating a pup if necessary. In case this pup was hypoglycemic (had low blood sugar), I brought a 12-cc syringe of dextrose with an 18-gauge needle. If I were at the Centre, to test for hypoglycemia I'd merely place a drop of the Seal's blood on a glucose meter and have the results in thirty seconds. In the wild, it's more of a judgment call. Symptoms may be as subtle as the pup's whiskers standing too erect, glassy unfocused eyes, or slight body tremors or twitching. Other times the pup may be unconscious and convulsing violently. If needed, dextrose is injected by inserting a one-inch needle between the vertebrae of the lower back, directly into the vein running inside the spine. Although it requires precision and concentration, it's a routine procedure. I usually begin treatments for the Seals at the location I find

d. gunn 97.

them, because starting the supportive care as soon as possible greatly increases the animal's chance of survival.

At our destination, we circumnavigated the island. Joe handled most of the paddling while I kept the binoculars glued to my face, scanning the shoreline. Decades of logging along the British Columbia and Washington coasts have left the beaches of the Gulf and San Juan Islands littered with driftwood, natural camouflage for a spotted pup lying still amid the debris. After our loop around the island, we beached the kayak and walked the one-mile circumference. No pup to be found. Had the pup's mother returned? That was the best scenario. It was either that or the little guy was frightened back into the water or a rising tide had washed it off the beach. Drizzle had turned to rain and as we turned for home, we were both thinking about what the pup—if its mother hadn't returned for it—must be going through. While it's true a Seal pup can survive days without nourishment before being rescued, too often an orphaned pup dies slowly and very much alone on some abandoned stretch of beach.

Except for the rain disturbing its surface, the ocean was calm, and Joe and I fell into a peaceful, synchronous paddling.

What was that? Abruptly, I stopped rowing. "Joe, I think I heard a pup," I said, not sure if it was just wishful thinking. We strained to take in every sound. It came again, and this time Joe heard it, too. We scanned the ocean surface in all directions; then I saw it. I pointed my paddle. "There it is, Joe, fifty yards straight ahead." We paddled slowly toward the pup, not wanting to alarm it. Drawing closer we could see it swimming frantically with its front flippers, holding its head out of the water and crying for mom. As we moved within ten feet of our target, our reluctant patient dove out of sight, only to resurface well behind us.

Joe turned the kayak towards the crying pup's new location, but I already had an idea of the fatal game this youngster was playing. Each time we approached, the frightened Seal dove and resurfaced well out of range. The situation seemed hopeless. I decided to mimic the mournful cries of the pup in a desperate attempt to lure it close. Wildlife impressions are not my strong suit, but it seemed to work. The pup responded, and with each call it swam closer. I moved to my knees with the net ready to enmesh my prey, while Joe readied himself to counterbalance my efforts. To overturn the kayak in this 55°F water would be disastrous.

As the pup came within range, my heart quickened. Suddenly it

dove and I watched him pass under the boat. My heart sank. How many more tries will we get, I wondered. The answer came quickly. Joe called my name and I turned. He pointed west—a very close west—and my gaze froze on a six-foot dorsal fin cutting through the water. "Killer Whale!" Joe shouted. He always did have a flair for the obvious.

We are accustomed to the pods of resident Orcas in these waters and they pose no threat to kayakers or seals. But this wasn't a resident pod. This was a lone, transient, Killer Whale, and a hungry loner would make a quick meal of a Seal pup. I had to work fast.

As calmly as I could, I resumed my impersonation and got the same encouraging response while Joe deftly maneuvered the kayak between the pup and the approaching Orca. Slowly the pup came closer. It was three feet off the left side of the kayak. The Killer Whale, 100 feet to the right, dove and disappeared. I plunged the net in and under the pup while Joe leaned out to counter my effort, then I jerked the loaded net towards my body and dropped the pup safely between my legs in the hold of the kayak. Seconds later the Orca surfaced again off our right side, condensation exploding from his blowhole. I was awestruck by his size, and the power of his breath resonated against my rib cage. He dove silently under the kayak, never showing himself to us again. As the kayak rocked in the Orca's wake, Joe and I slumped in our seats, unable to fully comprehend what we had just done.

Joe paddled homeward. I was busy with our neonatal passenger, who seemed determined to crawl up my legs and over the side. With a different agenda, I kept shoving him towards my feet. A kayak is no place for an examination, but I saw enough to grasp this Seal pup's problem. It was covered in a wet, white, fur coat called lanugo, which is normally shed by Harbour Seals in the uterus before birth. We had ourselves a preemie. No doubt rejected by its mother. Although not known for certain, it is believed that premature Harbour Seal pups

are abandoned at birth.

Back at the Wildlife Centre we began the routine intake procedure. Our new arrival was weighed. This was done by placing the pup on a plastic tray that had enjoyed a previous life on a bread

Jeff (LEFT) towel-dries a soaking wet Lumina. Young seal pup (TOP) nurses from its natural mom in the wild. A young volunteer (BELOW) learns to tube-feed an orphaned seal pup.

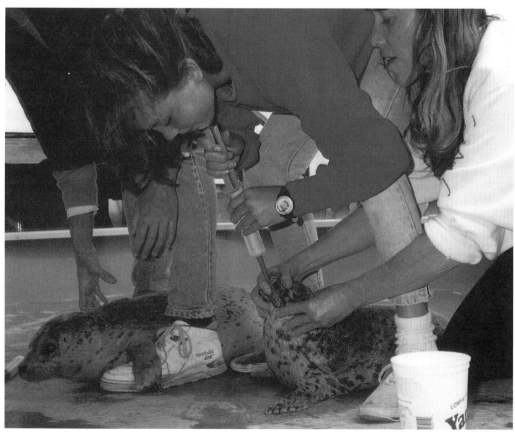

truck. The convenient device was suspended from a hanging scale. An average, full-term Harbour Seal weighs twenty-two to twenty-four pounds at birth. This one tipped the scale at seventeen pounds soaking wet. I administered four ounces of electrolytes through a tube directly into the stomach, a process the Seal quickly gets used to. A more thorough examination turned up nothing out of the ordinary. On the pup's underside, a genital slit indicated our orphan was a boy. In honor of Joe Luma's help with the rescue, we named him Lumina. In the morning, we would draw blood from the vein in the spine and send it to the lab for a complete workup. In the meantime, Lumina was placed in an empty bathtub where he quickly fell asleep. I expect he'd heard enough impersonations, and it was the authentic voices of the Seal pups around him that made him rest easy.

GROUNDED EAGLE

The Bald Eagle was exactly where he didn't want to be. On the ground. As we moved towards him from opposite sides, we could almost hear his heart pound. If the huge avian predator had been healthy, our approach would have driven him to fugitive flight. But, closing in on him, we gave him no choice. He had to stay and fight.

When in danger, an animal has two options—flight or fight. The first and most often chosen is the safest one, a hasty retreat from the threat. The second option, to fight, becomes necessary when the animal has no means of escape and must defend itself, its offspring, or its territory. It will also fight to maintain a desperately needed food source. The fight or flight response is more primal than a simple decision "should I stay or should I go." The stress triggering the response also initiates physical changes. These changes are intended to create maximum efficiency in the organs and muscles necessary for high energy output. The brain responds by stimulating the part of the nervous system responsible for voluntary actions such as flight, while another area of the brain increases strength and heart rate, routes more blood to the skeletal muscles, and increases blood glucose levels.

There were two of us and we approached slowly and steadily. The Eagle's eyes darted wildly from side to side, searching for a means of escape. I guessed his heart rate had accelerated to maximum. I knew mine had. Wings outstretched, body contour feathers fully erect, his blazing eyes cut to mine and held. Every inch of his quivering six-foot wingspan clearly said, "Don't mess with me." Unfortunately it was my job to mess with him, using all the high-tech equipment at my command: two wool blankets. My partner and I continued our stealthy march, she from the rear—holding one blanket in front of her like a wall so it appeared to be more of a barrier than a threat—and me from the front.

To avoid injury to the bird or ourselves, we knew the capture had to be fast and efficient. I stepped closer, saw him immediately shift his balance to his "heels." Positioned so, he could now unleash his talons with switchblade speed. Normally the Eagle would be more easily taken by the person approaching from the rear, but this day, because I was the more experienced, the dubious privilege fell to me.

I'd been told if an Eagle gets a grip on you, there's nothing you can do other than play dead and wait for it to release. I believed it because, on a number of occasions, I'd had smaller hawks take so firm a hold on my gloved hand that, to free myself, I had to slip my hand from the glove. Several hours later, when I checked their cages, they still had death grips on the glove. And a veterinarian I once

volunteered with told me of an Osprey that had sunk its talons so deeply into her arm, she had to anaesthetize the bird to effect her release. I try not to think of these things until after a capture.

I lunged with the blanket and as its shadow eclipsed the Eagle's world, I pressed him to the earth. It was easy to see where not to place my hands because in seconds the bird's powerful talons ripped

through the blanket in an attempt to free itself and do bodily injury to its attacker. I held fast and cautiously slipped one hand at a time under the blanket, gripping first one leg, then the other.

The Eagle was mine.

We immediately placed the terrified bird in a carrier, to be transported back to the Centre for diagnosis and treatment. By the time we pulled into the driveway, my pulse had returned to normal and my hands were no longer shaking from the rush of adrenaline. I doubted the Eagle's fight or flight response was as quick to abate. I placed the carrier in a secluded area, hoping the bird would calm somewhat before I began act two of his nightmare.

Although we make every effort to minimize stress on our captive patients, the level of horror experienced by wild animals, particularly birds, suddenly in the hands of humans is impossible to imagine. As quickly and quietly as I try to work, an examination takes a terrible toll in fear and distress. Every centimeter of the bird is pushed, probed, palpated, sniffed, exercised, and X-rayed. The eyes are looked into for

signs of blood or trauma. The ears are checked for blood and parasites. The inside of the mouth is examined for color and lesions. The breath is smelled for rotting food in the crop. Every bone is examined for fractures. Overall and specific feather quality is noted. The rectum and oil glands are checked for blockage. Feet are checked for broken talons, swelling, injuries, and leg strength. Blood is drawn from a vein under the wing. Full body and wing X rays are shot to locate any fractures or lead pellets in the digestive tract. Finally, a tube is slipped down the throat and into the stomach so that electrolytes may be administered to compensate for the dehydration that most of our patients are experiencing by the time they are found.

I can't think of a human experience to compare with this—except perhaps an alien abduction. Even after all this, the real clues to an animal's condition often become apparent only after it is placed outside in a safe, quiet enclosure and observed clandestinely.

As for our new patient, we were frustrated. Our physical examination yielded very little. The Eagle was dehydrated and starved, that was clear, but these conditions were secondary to a host of possibilities. However, as I'd hoped, careful observation of the bird in the outdoor enclosure gave me my first solid clues as to the cause of his suffering. Alone and feeling less threatened, the Eagle dropped his macho facade. The fierce avian warrior that just hours ago would have killed me for its freedom, fell into extreme lethargy. His head so low he was barely able to keep his beak off the ground, he held his wings up and out in what is referred to as a "tent posture." This behavior and the odd, unmistakable stance indicated an often fatal condition: lead poisoning.

This Eagle could have been a poster child for the state of our environment. Lead is an insidious toxin, working its way up through the food chain to bring those at the top a slow and miserable death.

The following day we took another blood sample, specifically to test for lead levels in the bird's blood. The results confirmed lethal levels of lead were indeed coursing through the veins of this magnificent creature.

We set to work. Our first efforts were directed to rehydrating the emaciated bird. A common result of starvation is a malfunctioning digestive system, so for the first twenty-four hours the Bald Eagle was tube–fed electrolytes. (If whole foods are fed to starving animals too soon, it can kill them.) Gradually we added liquefied salmon to the tube feedings, a sort of salmon smoothie. Eventually the Eagle graduated to whole salmon. For two weeks we gave our poisoned patient both conventional and homeopathic treatments for lead poisoning. Conventional treatment for lead poisoning consists of intramuscular injections of Calcium EDTA twice a day for two weeks. Calcium EDTA is a chelate, a compound that attracts metallic ions, pulling them out of body tissues into the bloodstream and allowing them to be excreted from the body in the urine. In homeopathy, like cures like, so the Eagle was given micro-doses of the same substance that initiated his symptoms. For lead poisoning, I used plumbum, otherwise known as lead.

This meant that twice a day I had to enter the Eagle's flight cage to capture and restrain the bird. We could see that the medication and remedies, combined with a steady, nutrient–rich diet, were working, as day by day the bird grew stronger. But as the neurological effects of the toxin wore off and the Eagle's strength approached a healthy norm, capture became more and more of a contest. The Eagle, obviously fed up with our program, became increasingly aggressive toward me.

Two weeks after treatments were discontinued, the time came for one final blood test. As usual, I entered the bird's domain, bolted the door behind me, and took several steps into the cage. But this time, one glance at the Eagle told me the power had shifted. His sharp eyes, capable of seeing a rabbit from a mile away, were not scanning side to side for an avenue of escape; they were fixed on me—as if I were prey. His bright, unblinking eyes held no fear. None. To him, now healthy and strong, I was no longer the dominant species. (This was one of those moments when I wondered why I hadn't gone to law school as my father insisted.)

Keeping my eyes diverted from the Eagle so as not to appear

threatening, I took two more steps in his direction. Big mistake. It was as if I had crossed a line the Eagle had drawn in the sand. From the far end of the flight cage he launched himself in my direction. The Eagle loomed, grew huge. I ducked, and the Eagle's flight feathers brushed the top of my head before he landed on the perch behind me. Cut off from the door, I turned to face the next attack. This time the Eagle came at me on a diagonal and backed me into the corner. I had no doubt this was exactly where he wanted me.

On the ground, the Eagle was no match for me, but in the air, the home court advantage was clearly on the avian side. He launched his next strike from across the width of the flight cage, hurling himself at me with outstretched talons. Fight or flight? I was in the same position the Eagle had been in only weeks before.

All I could do was turn away and bury my face in the wooden corner. An instant later I felt the weight of the vengeful bird hit my back, then ricochet off to land easily on a perch. I stood like stone. There was no searing pain and no torn flesh. I'd been given a reprieve. With a rusty, cackling voice, the Eagle flew to the far end of the flight, as if to say, "Now, get the hell out of here." I did just that.

Later, well after dark, I returned to the flight cage and found the

bird resting peacefully in the full moonlight. I hesitated, but like it or not, and I guessed neither of us did, this Eagle needed one last blood test. I crept toward him, about to yank the slumbering bird unceremoniously from his perch. I didn't feel good about it, but with any luck this would be the last time a human hand touched him.

When the perch was at eye level, I started raising my hands, inch by interminable inch, all the time watching those eagle eyes to make sure they didn't pop open. With one lightning grab, I grasped his legs and yanked him from his perch. I quickly drew the blood and got out of there. I  wasn't in the mood for another contest of wills.

Two days later the lab results were in. The Eagle's blood lead levels had returned to normal. This bird was one of the lucky few. He was found in time for treatment. Had he not been, our toxic environment would have claimed another wild life.

The time we had all worked so hard for had finally come. The two large doors on the flight cage were unbolted and swung wide open. With nothing between him and freedom, the bird didn't hesitate. We could hear the air being pushed by those giant wings as he glided through the doors. Six more wing beats and the Bald Eagle soared. We watched in silence as he flew out of sight, healthy and strong, ready to reclaim his piece of sky.

Foraging Behavior & Lead Poisoning

This eagle's inability to hold up its head and its wings held in a "roof" posture are indicative of lead poisoning.

Studies regularly support the theory that the feeding behavior of bald eagles is largely opportunistic. This means that whether they are eating live prey or carrion, eagles choose food that is easily available and vulnerable. Still, fish is preferred and in some areas waterfowl is a primary food.

Lead poisoning occurs so frequently among bald eagles that researchers are increasingly interested in their feeding habits. One explanation for secondary lead poisoning in bald eagles is the popularity of duck hunting in North America.

At some waters, shooting has been so prevalent that large amounts of spent lead shot accumulate in the sediment. Ducks, swallowing gravel to aid their digestive process, frequently ingest the lead pellets. Waterfowl also feed on aquatic plants growing in the toxic sediment.

Lead functions cumulatively as it breaks down in a duck's gizzard and becomes absorbed into the bloodstream via the intestinal walls. Once in the blood it degenerates the liver, kidneys, and nervous system. Even a few lead pellets in a duck's gizzard can be lethal. Although eagles often regurgitate the lead shot along with the feathers and bones of ducks they eat, the infusion of lead from prey's tissue and organs is unavoidable, and some lead enters the predator's gastrointestinal tract.

In 1991, the growing problem of lead poisoning inspired the mandatory use of steel shot on all federally owned waterfowl hunting areas in the United States. Still, the presence of lead in the environment will continue to threaten waterfowl and their predators for the foreseeable future.

And there are other contaminants.

In rivers, the presence of toxic chemicals like PCBs and mercury increases the likelihood fish have ingested these poisons and will pass them along to their predators. These concentrations of pollutants moving through the food chain pose a particular risk to top predators such as the bald eagle because they are subject to extraordinary doses of these poisons in a single meal.

Stephania Gaspari

BLACK FOX

As a wildlife rehabilitator, I am not only responsible for the care and well-being of the animals brought into my Centre, but to a small degree I also feel responsible for the emotional well-being of the people who accidentally injure an animal. Sure, there are those out there that can have a fawn bounce off their car like it was a bug on the windshield. I have had people trying to elicit my sympathies for the damage a deer has done to their 3,000-pound automobile. But more often than not, causing injury and suffering to an innocent creature is a traumatic experience—an experience that stays with some people for a lifetime. I have responded to accident calls, only to find an entire family sobbing by the side of the road. It is often difficult to know what to say to ease their guilt. Usually, just the fact that someone has arrived on the scene to care for the injured animal is a great comfort to the people involved.

On this particular evening, the female caller was quite distraught and incoherent. I was able to make out a location and the fact that she ran over something ... like a zebra. The sun had already gone down when I arrived at the scene. I pulled onto the shoulder behind a vehicle with emergency lights flashing and a lone occupant sitting behind the wheel. The driver was a woman in her early twenties. Her eyes were red and glassy, and her cheeks were streaked with mascara. She pointed off to the grass in front of her car and her tears once again began to flow. I approached the grassy area as quietly as I could. My flashlight illuminated one of the most beautiful animals I had seen. It was a black-phase Red Fox. It was immediately obvious why this animal is persecuted for its fur. It was also obvious that this animal had something terribly wrong with its lower torso. It was trying to escape my light by painfully dragging itself with its front paws. I estimated its weight and administered a sedative injection to ease its pain and panic.

The young woman insisted on returning to the Centre with me. Normally I would turn down such a request, but she was so emotionally wrapped up in this animal, I gave in. I placed the sedated Fox in a carrier and the three of us drove off into the night.

The first order of business was to stabilize the critical patient. The Fox was in deep shock. Her extremities were cold, her gums and tongue were deathly pale, and her respiration was shallow. I placed her on a warm heating pad on the examination table. There was no severe bleeding anywhere, although it was apparent she had a compound fracture of the rear leg—compound meaning that the bone was protruding through the skin.

I shaved a small patch of dense fur, inserted a needle into her vein, and started a slow flow of warm fluids to help alleviate her shocky condition. I administered homeopathic Arnica and Aconite for physical trauma and shock, then turned my attention to the fracture.

If it had not been for an occasional sniffle, I would have forgotten that Sarah was quietly watching from a dark corner.

I thoroughly cleaned the site of the fracture and removed small

bone chips, saving one large fragment just in case it became an important piece to the surgical puzzle. Since the bone end was exposed to the air, I covered it in a thick ointment to prevent it from drying out and thus creating another problem to face in surgery. A large padded bandage was placed on the leg as the last of the fluids dripped into the Fox's bloodstream. She was put away in a dark, warm cage for the night.

Sarah finally agreed to drive herself safely home, but she would call again in the morning.

The next morning the Fox was alert and stable, although I assumed she was in a fair amount of pain. I administered more Arnica to help relieve the pain.

I took the Fox to the local vet clinic where I am permitted use of

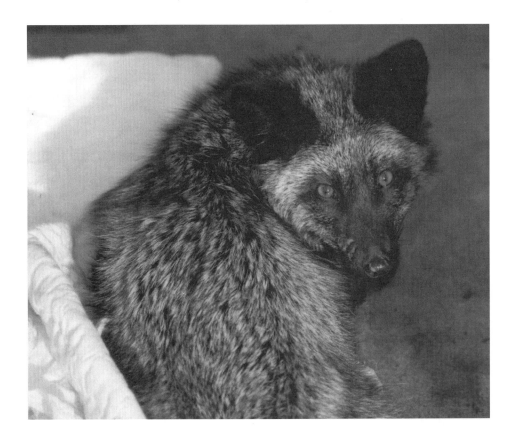

the X-ray facilities. Once the film was processed and dried, the extent of the Fox's injuries were visible. Besides the obvious compound fracture of the rear leg, the trained eye of the veterinarian identified a fracture to the pelvis. These were serious injuries and would require small, stainless steel plates to be fastened at the fracture sites. This was highly specialized surgery beyond the skills of our consulting vet. Also, the Fox's recovery would have to bring her back to her pre-accident level of athleticism or there would be no point in putting the animal through the surgery and painful recovery. Releasing a Fox with a handicap would probably be condemning it to starvation.

After making contact with a surgical specialist willing to donate his time, I couriered the Fox's X rays to him. The surgeon thought the prognosis for complete recovery was good, so surgery was scheduled. A private pilot flew my patient and me into the city, where I begrudgingly left the Fox at the surgical clinic and returned home. I am accustomed to staying very close to the animals in my care and participating in the surgery in some fashion. However, the clinic had a full, highly trained staff, so my presence would have been superfluous.

The surgery was the following morning and, from all reports, could not have gone better. The procedure took about five hours and resulted in a Fox that could no longer pass through an airport metal detector. The pelvis required two slender stainless steel plates and eight screws. The leg fracture necessitated the placement of a long plate and eleven screws. The Fox would spend a few days recovering under the staff's watchful eyes before being flown back to the Wildlife Centre. I was anxious to have her back in

my care, where I could continue stimulating her recovery with alternative medicine.

Back home again, caring for the Fox was routine. Changing the bandage on her leg daily and keeping her well fed were the highlights. As she began to feel a little better, she took exception to our fine bandage and began to chew it off. I needed a chewing deterrent and knew just where to find one. For those of you who have some experience with herbal tinctures, you know that some can be quite unpalatable. I set out to taste all of the tinctures in my medicine chest and came up with the foulest of the bunch.

Every day, the herbal tincture was wiped over the surface of the fresh bandage. The Fox went back to eating only what was presented in her food bowl.

While changing the bandage one morning, I became concerned by the lack of healing in the long leg incision. In fact, in a couple of places I was beginning to see a little stainless steel showing through. It was as if the metal were rejecting the skin that needed to cover it. We were unable to stop this unfortunate process and decided that another surgery was necessary. This time it would be a skin graft.

Once again the Fox was flown to the clinic. This procedure would not be a lengthy one, so I hung around in the background. The Fox was anaesthetized and the surgeon did a masterful skin graft over the area. The final stitches were being sewn into the leg and the anaesthetic had been turned off. We were all feeling quite optimistic when one of the technicians called out, "She's not breathing."

Those words made me panic like no others I have heard. One of the assistants began to breathe for the Fox through the tube that was still positioned in her trachea. We watched as the vet tech exhaled and the Fox's chest rose and dropped, rose and dropped. A chemical stimulant was placed under her tongue as her chest rose and dropped.

For the next twenty minutes, the Fox continued to breathe only as a response to the human breath being forced into her lungs. Finally, the surgeon softly spoke, "Okay, that's enough. She's gone."

Until the doctor broke the silence I had been so fixed on our patient that I was completely unaware of all the people in the operating room. Now, as I drew my attention away from our beautiful black Fox and looked around the room, I saw that there was not a single face that wasn't tear streaked. There was a young woman across from me taking this loss especially hard. She reminded me of a girl I saw a while back, sobbing behind the steering wheel of her car.

JAKE

It is a common belief that animals and beings in general share the goal of optimizing their existence. The force behind this dynamic process is natural selection of those who better adapt to their environment. The ultimate aim of animals is to pass on their genes to the next generations and to perpetuate life. This is easier said than done. Successful biological beings must develop successful strategies which enable them to survive and cope with the environment and with problems such as finding food and mates to reproduce.

Knowing an animal's food requirements and eating habits is critical in wildlife rehabilitation because we must be capable of sustaining any one of hundreds of species on demand. Is the animal a vegetarian or meat eater? Does it eat insects, plants, seeds, bark, fish, carrion, birds, snails, or a host of other difficult-to-find menu items? How does it forage and eat. It may eat live food only, caught on the wing. It may probe down into the mud or burrow for insects. It is very possible that the food presented to it in captivity is not even recognized as food.

Food requirements are as disparate as the animals themselves. While one creature may be a highly specialized feeder, eating only live food, others have a more varied, opportunistic palate. Available food sources and feeding strategies also determine whether the animal is a solitary or a group feeder. Concentrated food resources are more likely to attract group feeders, while sparsely distributed food tends to attract the solitary feeder.

Rodents account for nearly forty percent of all mammal species and, in part, owe their biological success to their unique feeding equipment. Their chisel-like incisors allow them to exploit food sources not available to other animals. They can feed on the toughest bark, crack open the hardest nuts, and generally access vegetation inaccessible to other mammals.

This story is an account of my first experience with a rodent that is rather challenging to handle and rehabilitate safely: a Porcupine. The Porcupine is best known for its 30,000 needle-like quills. Each pointed quill has a series of overlapping barbs which cause the quill to work its way deeper and deeper into the flesh of any unfortunate predator. The Porcupine, however, is not without its enemies. It is successfully preyed upon by the fisher, wolverine, coyote, fox, cougar, and great horned owl. In this particular case, the Porcupine fell victim to that most prolific predator, the automobile.

The injured Porcupine was delivered to us, unconscious, in a cardboard box. I leave to your imagination what happens to an animal weighing no more than thirty pounds, caught between a set of Firestones and hard pavement.

The staff at the Centre christened our new patient Jake, and we quickly set about making him well, but how exactly does one go about handling and rehabilitating this prickly animal? This being my first experience with one, I wasn't completely sure, so I stuck to the basics. Jake's condition was grim; his wounds were ugly and severe. Wanting to take full advantage of his unconscious state, we worked as quickly as possible. Our first task was to clean and suture the encrusted wounds. As far as we could tell there were no broken bones, but his two beaver-like front teeth were snapped off at the gum line. Judging from his state of unconsciousness, I assumed he'd suffered head trauma. We would have to wait and see. In the meantime, I treated him for shock, started a course of antibiotics, and put him away in a warm, quiet cage.

By morning Jake was on his feet and as alert as an injured nocturnal mammal could be. He was very unsteady—I suspected his head injury caused this—and he was obviously in pain. What he needed now was rest. Knowing privacy and fresh air would calm this innately solitary animal, we carried his cage outside to a large, natural enclosure and left his cage door open. I left an assortment of soft food items for him; apple, corn, leafy branches, tender inner bark, and plenty of fresh water. The enclosure also contained a wooden den box he could trade for his cage if he chose to.

Twenty-four hours later, Jake hadn't eaten anything. I left him different fruit, different leafy branches, and different bark. He still didn't eat. If he didn't start—and soon—we'd have to tube-feed him. I knew this procedure would be traumatic for such a badly injured animal—not to mention his caregivers. In a last-ditch effort, we left an assortment of children's breakfast cereals and a slice of fruit pie. We waited.

Jake was eating again! It might be Captain Crunch and cherry pie, but he was eating.

Over the next few weeks, his wounds healed with no sign of

infection. But examining him was always touch and go. Or should I say touch and run? When approached, Jake often turned threatening, turning his back to us and thrashing his quill-laden tail. It was a threat we all took seriously. We knew Porcupines couldn't actually throw their quills, so when Jake was feeling hostile we simply kept a safe distance.

Once, in our efforts to elude Jake's menacing tail, we mistakenly trapped him under a blanket. I say mistakenly because when we removed the blanket, hundreds of barbed quills came with it. Poor Jake was a walking piece of Velcro. Fortunately the quills are loosely attached and grow back quickly. This incident reminded

Although not without natural predators, the porcupine's best chance for survival is to stay away from highways.

me again how much of what we learn in wildlife rehabilitation comes from our mistakes. Hopefully we never cause unnecessary suffering, and we certainly never make the same mistake twice.

As time went on, Jake and I became used to one another and it became easier to examine him. I discovered he liked to have his chest and stomach scratched. To encourage it he would stand on his back legs and rest his front legs on my hand. Sometimes, when the scratching felt especially good, his back leg would strum a guitar the way a dog's does.

Gradually we managed to introduce more nutritious foods to Jake's junk-food diet. His front teeth were growing back, but he was still uncertain on his feet, taking eight or ten steps forward, then two wobbling steps to the side. Occasionally the two sideways steps were replaced by an awkward fall. Unhappily, we recognized that if this was the extent of Jake's recovery, he couldn't be released. To do so would be his death sentence.

Jake's mellow disposition and his diminishing fear of humans made him a good candidate for permanent placement at another facility. But first I had to find one.

My investigation turned up a zoo in Chicago that was looking for a male Porcupine. As it happened, I was planning a trip to that area, so I dropped in at the zoo to inspect Jake's prospective new home. Perfect.

The intended enclosure, in the children's zoo, was large and beautifully landscaped. Besides the assortment of native Midwestern trees, shrubs, and grasses, it housed some pheasants and, best of all, a resident female Porcupine. I knew Jake would be happy here. Arrangements were made, airfare was booked, and Jake flew off to the Windy City.

As with all new arrivals, Jake was kept in isolation for several weeks to ensure he didn't bring disease into the healthy captive population. About a week after his arrival, I received a call from the zoo. Jake wasn't eating and they were worried. A urine analysis showed high levels of organic compounds known as ketones, an indication of starvation. The concerned keeper rattled off a list of foods both natural and manufactured that she'd tried. Jake would touch none of it.

"Wrong diet," I told her.

"But this is what captive porcupines eat," she replied, somewhat defensively.

"Jake's waiting for cereal and pastry," I said. "Specifically, Captain Crunch and cherry pie."

While she didn't sound convinced, she must have given it a try because the next and last time I heard from the zoo, Jake was eating and they'd moved him from isolation to his new enclosure, where he quickly became a favorite of the staff and visitors.

One small problem. The docents—volunteers responsible for public education—were having a tough time explaining to the children why there was cherry pie in the Porcupine habitat.

ON THE ROCKS

From the bluff above the rocky shore I scanned the coastline for the reported pup. A limp, gray-colored pup draped across the gray rocks is very easily overlooked. It was getting to be late in the day, with fading winter light, and the weather looked like it was taking a nasty turn. It was mid-November, and when the sun shines it can be quite pleasant, but when the sun goes down it is just plain damp and cold.

Something that looked like it might be a stranded pup caught my eye. I worked my way along the edge of the bluff to a better vantage point. Yep, that was a Harbour Seal pup. Whether or not it was still alive was impossible to say from up here. It just looked like so much waterlogged debris, rejected by the surf. Assuming that this was not an orphaned pup, weaning would have taken place four to six weeks after birth. At that time it was up to the pup to learn to forage successfully—or end up like this guy, who had become the focus of my attention.

I figured the quickest route to him was straight down, by rope. Once I reached the rocks below, I planned to pick him up, work my way along the rocky shore to a section of flat beach, and wait for the

Centre's Zodiac to pick us up. I'd come back for my truck later. I called the Centre, advised them of the situation, and gave them the location. They'd leave immediately, they said. ETA? About an hour.

I shrugged into my backpack—my version of a country doctor's black bag—tied the rope to the trailer hitch on my truck, and threw it over the side. After giving the rope a couple of hard, precautionary tugs, I got into position. Crawling backward on all fours, I inched my way over the edge and started down. With no rock-climbing experience, what I was doing was about as close to rappelling as drowning is to swimming.

During my descent I felt the wind turning harsh. Looking down about thirty feet, I could see the prostrate pup. The surf was beginning to pound the rocks a little and, looking up, I could see only sky. "What in the world do I think I'm doing out here?" I thought to myself. I half expected to see my life passing before my eyes. Pushing back the wave of panic that was trying to glue me to that spot, I loosened my grip and continued down.

It took a few seconds for my hands to release after my feet hit solid rock. I was down and I was feeling pretty pleased with myself. I glanced around. Behind me was a shallow cave and in front of me, on the rocks, lay the ailing pup.

I dropped my pack and spread a blanket on the higher ground in the mouth of the cave. By the time I picked up the pup, the waves were already threatening his resting place. I set him down on the

blanket carefully and for the first time got a good look at him. It wasn't encouraging. He looked in critical condition: underweight, unconscious, convulsing, with open-mouthed, squeaky respiration. I had to hurry and get him to the flat beach area I'd spotted from the bluff. I could work on him there while I waited for the Zodiac.

I stood to scope out our escape route, but all I saw was rock and water, behind me a sheer cliff and on three sides the wind-whipped ocean. Evidently between the incoming tide and the incoming wind, what was to be my rocky retreat was now just more ocean. I was cut off from the beach.

For a moment I completely forgot about the unconscious pup as my mind raced through various scenarios, all of which in the end still left me standing here. Once again that feeling of panic that never seems to be too far away started moving in. This time it was chased away by the sound of an outboard motor. The Zodiac was coming for me. For us.

It was quickly turning into the kind of evening not recommended to be out in a small boat. As the Zodiac tried to move in close, the surf lifted it up and threatened to smash it back down on the rocks. I could hear the motor strain as they turned back into the wind and put some distance between themselves and me.

Knowing the water rescue was out, I turned my attention back to the Seal pup. I was sure I would have company on the bluff above in a little while.

The pup's convulsions looked to be caused by hypoglycemia, a condition often resulting from severe emaciation and dehydration. I dug into my pack and pulled out a pouch of intravenous fluids, heat packs, a jar of sterile liquid dextrose, some needles, and a couple of syringes. (Squeezing the heat packs ruptures an inner packet, causing a chemical reaction that produces the necessary heat to warm the IV fluids before they enter the bloodstream.) I filled a 12-cc syringe with a mixture half dextrose and half IV fluids, then inserted the needle between two lumbar vertebrae in the unconscious Seal's lower back, into a vein running the length of the spine inside the vertebrae.

Before the syringe was empty of the dextrose, the convulsions stopped and the pup was awake and vocalizing. I wrapped the long slender tube attached to the IV fluid pouch several times around the heat pack, removed the glucose syringe, and connected the needle to the IV tubing. As the warm fluids entered the Seal's circulatory system, I forced a sturdy stick into a crack in the rock wall above the pup's head and hung the IV pouch. Gravity kept the fluids flowing.

The exhausted pup made a good patient, resting quietly, letting the fluids begin the process of rehydrating his dehydrated tissues. I took a moment to stand and stretch, then stared at the churning waves.

When the phone in my pack rang, I figured it was for me. It was one of my colleagues on the bluff. From my end it was a short conversation. "Uh-huh. We're doing fine . . . No, I don't have any idea what to do now . . . Yes, I know the coast guard could lift me out, but do you want to tell the Centre's board of directors we owe the coast guard $10,000 for a Seal rescue? . . . No, I didn't think so . . . I don't think the water will get much higher. I'm thinking we can spend the night here and the Zodiac can get us at dawn . . . Yes I know I never get up that early . . . Do me a favor. Have someone come back and drop me a sleeping bag and a picnic basket. Don't forget water . . . No, I have everything I need for the pup. Thanks."

We were alone again. I administered some homeopathic remedies for the pup's severe respiratory troubles and sat back against the cliff to enjoy a granola bar, the company, and the long night ahead. A light rain had started to fall, which seemed to cause the wind to die down.

The pup was still conscious, so I decided it was safe to administer oral fluids. This is done by slipping a long tube through the mouth directly into the stomach. The fluids are then passed from a very large syringe into the tube into the stomach. This operation is quick, painless, and standard procedure for all pups that are not yet eating whole fish on their own. If you have ever seen the size of the fish that these pups swallow whole, you can see why swallowing this narrow tube is rather uneventful. As long as the pup

Orphaned seal pups "hauled-out" on a wooden platform.

remained conscious, I planned to give him four ounces of fluids every two hours. Virtually all emaciated, dehydrated animals are given nothing but fluids for the first twenty-four hours as death from dehydration is a greater risk than death from starvation.

The clouds were beginning to break up and a hint of moonlight was illuminating their fringe. I could hear many other animals out there in the darkness. Great horned owls announced their presence to each other as they hunted for the overly abundant rabbits. There was a repeated splashing out in the water, and a playful grunting sound I knew to be river otters. Every now and then I heard the breathing of what I presumed to be a Harbour Seal

These wild seals have hauled themselves onto a sandy beach.

surfacing nearby. It was truly magical. The pup was wrapped in the blanket and appeared to be sleeping quietly. I was warm in the sleeping bag, wondering back in time. I was trying to trace the events that led me to be sharing this rock with an alien species. I don't mean the events of today, but where in my life did I turn right instead of left? What innocent and spontaneous decision did I make ten years ago that was responsible for my being on these rocks tonight?

I woke to a predawn sky, a calm morning, and the sound of the Zodiac's outboard motor. Time to go home.

Because of his unseasonably late arrival at the Centre, we named the pup Tardy. Despite my efforts of the night before, Tardy was still in critical condition. He was lethargic, his breathing was labored, and there were numerous deep puncture wounds on his lower torso and tail area, all infected. As I carefully turned him to get a closer look, his front flippers trembled, indicating the little fellow was in considerable pain.

Whenever he opened his eyes, which wasn't often, they oozed pus, and large amounts of it ran down his cheeks. His corneas were grayish-blue and opaque. Pus and blood also seeped from his nostrils, a bad sign indicative of heavy lungworm infestation. We had this confirmed by a fecal sedimentation exam, which also showed Tardy was host to roundworms. It is very common for a Seal in this situation to die from lungworm infestation and verminous pneumonia.

Compounding Tardy's condition was the lateness of the season and the colder-than-normal weather. The seal facilities were outdoors, and by now the pools were frozen and the outdoor plumbing drained and shut off. Tardy was skin and bones, and I knew he wouldn't survive another night outside. So we became roommates. He was not an ideal house guest.

For three weeks, Tardy lived in my bathtub. Every night I went to sleep to the sounds of a marine mammal in the next room. Every morning I awoke to the smell. And trust me, you've never truly experienced bathtub ring until you've had a resident Seal in your tub. Tardy's treatment continued immediately upon his arrival at the Centre. On the homeopathic front, I gave him Cinchona (Peruvian bark) as it helps an animal recover quickly from the loss of vital fluids caused by dehydration, bleeding, burns, vomiting, and diarrhea. I also tube-fed him an electrolyte solution with a specially formulated herbal lung tincture, cleaned his puncture wounds, and started a course of antibiotics. I planned to start lungworm treatment the next day.

The following morning Tardy's condition was relatively unchanged, with the very notable exception of the brown diarrhea flipper-painted all over my tub.

I suspected Tardy's deep puncture wounds were the result of a dog attack. To avoid further complications from the cuts and to relieve his discomfort, I placed some homeopathic Ledum (Marsh-Tea) under his tongue. Not long after its application, the trembling in Tardy's flippers stopped and he seemed to relax.

Lungworm infestations are dangerous to any animal, and Tardy had a severe case. For lungworm, conventional drugs are best, but there are risks. Worming drugs are strong, and the mass die-off of worms can bring on anaphylactic shock and kill the host animal. To forestall shock and protect Tardy, I injected him with steroids for a couple of days before and after worming.

To further stimulate his recovery, I had to get Tardy swimming. While my bathtub kept him safe, it didn't allow for physical activity. I found an abandoned Jacuzzi tub about twice the size of my bathtub, filled it with warm water outdoors, and slipped Tardy into the water. For several minutes he paddled around the pink pool, showing instinctive movement patterns, but when fatigue and shivering set in, I quickly returned him to his apartment. In the days following, I lengthened the swimming sessions and, much to Tardy's delight, started tossing in some thawed herring. Tardy quickly positioned each fish head first in his mouth and sucked it out of sight. There was nothing wrong with the guy's appetite.

Tardy was now twenty-five pounds. Although he still didn't have the layer of fat necessary to thermoregulate, he could not be expected to continue his recovery in a bathtub.

The Centre procured a clear plastic dome and installed it over the twelve-foot outdoor pool, adding an electric heater to warm the air in the pool enclosure. We hung a heat lamp over the wooden haul-out platform in the centre of the pool and broke and removed the surface ice. Tardy moved in the next day.

Now Tardy could swim at will, eat all his fish in the water, and haul himself out under the heat lamp whenever he wanted to. To be safe, and because of the unrelentingly cold weather, I still tucked him into my tub at night.

I watched his eyes carefully and for the first time began to see clearing in his corneas. The corneas do not slowly become transparent. Rather, the opaqueness begins to retreat, like a window shade being pulled away—first from the top of the eyeball and slowly from the sides.

By Christmas day, Tardy was forty-one pounds and no longer spent his nights in my apartment. The water in his pool was 45°F, and he tolerated it fine. He began to look like a fat, healthy sausage.

As the winter days went by, his corneas continued to improve, a fecal examination for parasites was negative, and his weight hit fifty-seven pounds. But before he could be set free, Tardy needed a week or two of exercise in the eighteen-foot pool. There was one problem. The ice covering its surface was eight inches thick. After ruling out several hare-brained schemes to thaw the pool, two volunteers and I spent six hours fracturing the ice and hauling it up a ramp, where we tossed it over the side. Tardy's new pool was ready. We hoped Tardy was.

No problem. He took to the big pool immediately: a few easy laps around the circumference, then down to the bottom for a nap. Although the water was a frigid 40°F, he rarely hauled himself out. A

week later, Tardy's weight leveled off at fifty-nine pounds. It was time to set him free.

After I attached a plastic ID tag to his hind flipper, we put him into the back of an enclosed pickup truck and returned to the general location of his stranding. On the way there, I caught more than a few quizzical looks from other drivers when Tardy ogled them from the back window.

We unloaded Tardy on a sheltered beach, placing him on the sand near the water. He stared out at the surf for a moment, looked back in my direction, and then he was gone.

Driving back to the Centre, I daydreamed, imagining Tardy could communicate his experiences to other Seals. He'd have a story to tell. That was certain. But who'd believe it?

PSYCHO

When working with wildlife, it's important to keep an emotional distance. Our patients are not pets, and I stress this with both staff and volunteers. They may be cute but they may not be cuddled. Our job is to prepare them for a return to the wild with their feral instincts intact. Emotional distance, that was the rule. But sometimes an animal comes along and begs you to break that rule, and a bond is formed. This was one of those times.

It was early summer and baby bird season was in full swing. At a large rehab centre this can lead to an influx of thousands of orphaned and injured birds. Some are old enough to self-feed, but most of the young need to be hand-fed every twenty to forty minutes—dawn till dusk. A few shifts of this and you develop great admiration for the role a mother bird plays.

This particular season brought an unusually large number of injured and starving Crows. Crows always seem to suffer a lot of abuse out in the world. For those of you who have never taken the time to sit back and observe Crows in the wild, you don't know what you are missing. They are wonderful birds with complex personalities.

Our Crows were housed indoors about six to a cage. Feeding these guys cage-after-cage, day-after-day, they became somewhat of a blur, with each Crow looking pretty much like the others. Except for one.

Utterly fearless and sure of himself, his cocky posturing fairly shouted, "Hey, I'm not with these guys." His brashness and confidence made me certain he'd been raised by humans from a young age. This worried me because early and intense contact with humans—and no contact with its own species—often leads to an animal that can't survive in the wild. And the wild was exactly where these birds were headed—and soon.

As the season wore on, the bird became a favorite of the volunteers, and he was frequently allowed loose in the nursery while we tended our patients. If during the course of the day you happened to drop a pencil or a small feeding syringe, our ebony friend delighted in coming from nowhere to snatch it, then danced back and forth in front of you, chewing on his prize. Retrieving it was near to impossible. If you grabbed for him, he'd quickly hop under a cage or dart behind a table in a Crow version of "keep-away." Many times I'd look down to catch him untying my shoelace or pulling all the canned goods off the lower shelves. This devilish behavior earned him the name Psycho. And it fit.

One evening when I was working late, I heard a strange voice chattering in the next room. Upon investigating, I found only Psycho. He'd taken to mimicking. And he applied himself to the task with such determination that what started as a couple of words grew to six or eight by summer's end.

The end of summer meant it was time to release the Crows. It was

also time for me to prepare for my move to a new wildlife centre in the Pacific Northwest. And while my future was bright and challenging, Psycho's looked dim.

In most cases, animals that can't survive on their own and can't be released are euthanized. This has always been the most difficult part of my work. Philosophically, I agree a wild animal is better off dead than living a life in captivity or slowly starving to death in the wild, but the decision to kill an animal, even for its own good, is always tough. And I just couldn't bring myself to kill Psycho—or let anyone else do it. So I looked at the alternative and decided to take it. I'd steal him.

On my last morning at the Centre, my pickup, its bed filled with my possessions, was parked out front. The moment was now. I grabbed Psycho from his enclosure, popped him into the get-away cage next to the driver's seat, and the two of us hit the open road. So Psycho could see where we were going, I sat his cage on top of a box of books. Whenever I glanced over at him, he appeared mesmerized by the world whizzing by.

It was predicted the day would be Southern California hot, so I'd taken along a spray bottle of water to keep him cool. Most birds like to be misted. Not Psycho. I'd spray and he'd scream, "Stop it. Stop it. Hello, Jeff."

That night, late, we checked in at a motel just off the highway. A queen-sized bed for me. For Psycho I pulled the desk chair into the middle of the room, spread newspaper around its base, then let him out of his cage to perch on the chair back. While he seemed content enough with this arrangement, by the time I came out of the bath-room he was doing laps on my bed, daring me to capture him. Eventually I did and we both settled down for the night.

Sleep came quickly and morning even quicker. While I showered, Psycho preened on his chair-back perch. I didn't hear the housekeep-er knock and when I didn't respond, she obviously assumed the room was empty and opened the door. A startled Psycho took flight, head-ing straight toward sunlight and endless blue skies.

Psycho possessed none of the skills necessary to survive in the wild: his ability to fly was minimal due to an old wing injury; he had never foraged for a wild diet; he was unaware of predators; and worst of all, to his mind, humans were both hospitable and friendly. I dressed in double-time and set out to find him.

There was a park located near the motel, so I focused my search there. By the time I decided to take a lunch break, my neck was stiff from looking up into the trees. I returned to the park with my carry-outs, most of which I used to salt the area. In a matter of minutes I was surrounded by Pigeons, Sparrows, and Crows, none of which looked even slightly familiar.

Afternoon turned to evening. I knew it was only a bird, but I felt such an overwhelming sense of loss; I decided I would extend my stay one more day.

The next morning I woke to what I thought was someone calling my name. I stuck my head out the door and listened intently. I couldn't tell where it was coming from, but this time I heard it clearly. "Hello Jeff."

I was dressed and outside in the parking lot in an instant, scan-ning in all directions and listening hard for that screech of a voice I'd grown so fond of.

"Hello, Jeff. Que pasa?" (There was a large Hispanic contingent at the Centre). My ears led my eyes to a point about thirty feet up a tree whose branches fanned out over the parking lot. At the end of a stout branch, dancing back and forth and chattering incessantly, was Psycho.

Without giving a thought to what I'd do when I reached him, I began to climb. I was lucky. The tree was of a width to wrap my arms around, and there were solid footholds and well-placed branches. I kept my eyes on Psycho, not sure of what he'd do next, but he seemed delighted to have me at his level and stayed in place. With one well-timed, very fast grab, I had him—or he let me have him. I was never sure which. But it felt great to hit the road again with Psycho next to me. Next stop, Puget Sound. Another six or eight hours on the road, a couple of hours waiting in line for the ferry, and our journey was over.

I hoped my arrival, Crow in tow, wouldn't raise too many eyebrows. I left it to Psycho to make his place there, and he did, capturing the hearts of everyone at the Centre. His new home was in a protected corner against a shed. Although he was kept in a large cage, Psycho spent hours running about and poking around in the grass. His forte was playing catch. I could toss a grape or a stick from fifteen feet away and Psycho would catch it—though he never did grasp the idea of relinquishing the item so the game could continue.

Psycho's cage became a favorite stop on the Centre's educational tours, and he reveled in the attention. He put on a good show, particularly for kids, who'd linger outside his cage, pointing and laughing at his wild antics. Psycho showed them Crows possessed both intelligence and charm—and that they weren't the pests and vermin their reputations made them out to be. Psycho was an ambassador for Crows everywhere.

One quiet summer night, after all the animal work had been done, I was relaxing in my apartment over the treatment centre. Suddenly, through the open window, I heard Psycho's shrill voice screaming for attention with an urgency that made my hair stand on end.

I ran downstairs, grabbed a flashlight, and flew out the back door. Running full tilt, I pointed the beam of light toward Psycho's cage. It was tough to focus while running over rough ground, but the light quickly exposed the ugly reality of Psycho's plight. I yelled like a wild man while continuing my charge toward the helpless Crow.

An enormous Great Horned Owl appeared to be attached to the side of Psycho's cage. In its talons, flush against the cage and held by his throat, was Psycho. The Owl was trying to pull him through the bars. I guessed a sleepy Psycho had perched too close to the cage's outer side, making him irresistible prey to the island's fiercest nocturnal predator.

I was almost on top of the Owl, my screaming banshee attack by now a full-throated roar, before it dropped Psycho and flew into a nearby tree. I threw open the cage door, dropped the flashlight, sank to my knees, and gently picked up Psycho. His body rested limply in my hands. He took a couple of shallow breaths, gave my finger a little bite, and was gone.

That night Psycho rested in a shoebox beside my bed. The next morning I took him into the woods and buried him, along with some of his favorite toys and his water dish. Today, when I see Crows, they always make me smile and they always make me think of Psycho.

And when I remind the Centre's new recruits not to get emotionally attached to our patients, I feel just the tiniest bit hypocritical.

STRANDED TURSIOPS

Just after sunrise, a vacationing tourist jogging down the beach came face to face with her first Dolphin. Realizing the seriousness of the situation, she sprinted back to her bungalow to awaken her traveling companion.

Waking up at dawn was not my idea of a vacation. However, when I heard about the stranded Dolphin, all was forgiven. I went to find our resort manager to scrounge a few first aid supplies, while my other half began working the telephone in an attempt to locate a stranding network representative.

No one knows for certain why Dolphins become stranded. One theory says geomagnetic disturbances on the earth's surface short circuit the Dolphin's navigational systems, inadvertently pointing them toward land. Another assumption is they simply venture too far into shallow water in pursuit of prey. But generally, the lone Dolphin is stranded due to illness.

Life-threatening forces come to play on an aquatic mammal imprisoned out of its element. Stress plays heavily on all its physiological systems. Hormones such as cortisol are released from the adrenal cortex into the circulatory system. Sustained high levels of this hormone inevitably have a deleterious effect on the animal's immune system.

Too long out of the water and the animal's body weight, no longer buoyant, becomes a factor; gravitational forces cause labored breathing and cardiac stress. A Dolphin will begin to dehydrate, and because it is unable to thermoregulate, even on a cloudy day, hyperthermia will cook the animal. Exposure to the sun quickly worsens the animal's condition by blistering its sensitive, unprotected skin.

By the time I returned with the necessary supplies—a bucket, towels, a thick white ointment (zinc oxide), and a shovel—the marine mammal folks had been alerted and were on their way. I added my homeopathic remedy kit to my load and my friend and I hurried back to the suffering cetacean. (Cetaceans are the order of marine mammals that includes whales, dolphins, and porpoises.)

Amazingly for so early in the morning, a small group of people had already gathered around the stranded animal, an event sure to increase its anxiety and stress level. I explained this to a couple of bystanders and asked them to keep the curious onlookers at a comfortable distance.

Then we went about trying to make the Dolphin as comfortable as possible and prevent any further damage we could.

I crushed some homeopathic remedies and poured the powder inside the Dolphin's lip.

One remedy, Cinchona or Peruvian bark, was to help counter the debilitating effects of dehydration, and the other, cheladonium majus, was to stimulate liver function. It is not uncommon for a stranded cetacean to show signs of vascular collapse. Blood pools in the animal's body, and with circulation effective only to the heart and brain, the rest of the body is basically bypassed. Organs such as the liver are impaired, and toxic compounds normally metabolized reach dangerous levels.

To reduce pressure on the Dolphin's anatomy and allow the animal to rest in a more natural position, we dug holes in the sand under its pectoral flippers. We kept the holes filled with cold water to allow excess body heat to dissipate and—careful not to obstruct the blow hole—draped wet towels across the Dolphin's body. We flushed the Dolphin's eyes with sea water to keep them clean and moist. I knew I had to do the same for its blow hole. I waited until just after respiration, when the blow hole closes, then poured water across the area. After applying a thick coat of zinc ointment to any of the animal's skin exposed to the sun, we asked people in front of the animal's view to move out of its visual range. There was nothing to do now except wait for the troops to arrive and keep the towels wet.

The volunteers from the stranding network showed up about an hour later. I think they were quite shocked to discover all immediate care procedures were in place, but they were also efficient. They quickly evaluated the situation and decided to transport the animal to a nearby rehabilitation facility. They laid a large modified stretcher down next to the Dolphin and, rolling the animal from one side to the other, deftly manipulated the stretcher under him. It was a pitiful sight as the Dolphin was carried away on a stretcher.

With the Dolphin safe on a thick foam pad in the back of a truck, one of the volunteers came back and invited my partner and myself for a tour of their rehab facility. While I quickly accepted the invitation, my partner opted to return to her jogging.

The facility was as large and modern a rehabilitation centre as I'd ever seen. There were deep fiberglass pools forty or fifty feet in diameter, a huge electric crane for lifting animals in and out of the water, and the food prep area was as pristine and shiny as my mother's kitchen. There was also a blood lab, a portable X-ray unit, and a large staff of veterinarians and trained volunteers. As envious as I was of their facility, I didn't envy their survival statistics. In all fairness, stranded Dolphins are generally in such dire straits by the time they wash up on shore that restoring them to health is a formidable task.

When they began the examination of their newest patient, I was invited to sit in. As the examination progressed, I saw what was, in my opinion, one of the reasons for their low success rate.

The Dolphin was placed pool side on a double thick foam pad, where the terrified animal was immediately surrounded by people, each doing a specific job. While some restrained the Dolphin to prevent injuries to the animal or staff, others wheeled in and positioned the portable X-ray unit. Blood was drawn, a urine sample was taken, X rays were shot, an ultrasound examination was conducted, an endoscope was inserted down the esophagus for a view of the first of its three stomachs, stomach contents were flushed out, fluids were tubed in, and a course of broad spectrum antibiotics was begun.

For a human with some understanding of what was being done and why, this would be a stressful examination. To a species out of its element and with no understanding of human intentions, it induces stress of a dangerous magnitude. At a time when a sick animal most needs a strong immune system, stress, medical procedures,

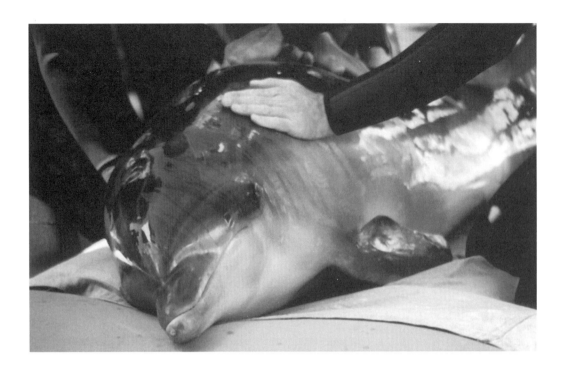

captivity, human handling, and isolation from its own species work only to compromise its innate healing force.

After the examination, the Dolphin was lowered by crane into the strangest body of water that marine mammal had ever experienced. Round and round the confused Dolphin swam in lethargic clock-wise circles. Every so often, its rostrum, or snout, collided with the sides of its aquatic prison.

After the frenzy of admitting and examining the new patient had passed, I introduced myself to the head veterinarian and was pleased to learn she knew of my alternative treatments with seals from some articles I'd had published. When she said she looked forward to discussing this Dolphin with me, I barely contained my excitement. Truth was, I'd been waiting a long time to utilize my treatments with a Dolphin.

The information gleaned from the morning medical assault served mostly to eliminate what wasn't wrong; there was no firm diagnosis. The information shared with me was that the Dolphin was considerably underweight, respiration was shallow and raspy sounding, and it was bloated to the point it couldn't stay submerged. There were also a lot of digestive sounds. Finally, it had coughed up lungworms, frequently a secondary condition to whatever is causing the animal's debilitation. The Dolphin's symptoms were strikingly similar to those in many harbour seals I treat.

I decided to make some suggestions and sought out the veterinarian. She already had the animal on antibiotics, but the Dolphin's immune system needed to be supported with herbal tinctures. I recommended Echinacea and Astragalus. Echinacea not only kills a broad range of dangerous viruses and bacteria, it contains a natural broad spectrum antibiotic. Astragalus enhances the immune system when it is depressed by blood deficiency, weakness, and fatigue. The respiratory distress would benefit from herbs and a well-chosen homeopathic remedy, and the severe bloating was also homeopathically treatable.

The veterinarian, skeptical about my claims of how dynamically these treatments would reduce the bloating, was also concerned that given the animal's weakened state, the bloating might be the only thing keeping it afloat. But she agreed to give my methods a try.

As a precaution, four volunteers stationed themselves pool side, ready to enter the water and keep the Dolphin afloat if need be. The first dose of the oral remedy for bloating (Club moss) resulted in not much more than a few Dolphin farts. Several hours later I repeated the remedy—with very different results. The surface of the pool erupted in an endless stream of bubbles and fecal material. It was as if the

Dolphin were deflating like a punctured beach ball. Slowly the Dolphin's dorsal fin dropped below the surface for the first time, as the animal gently came to rest on the bottom of the pool.

The tension among the volunteers was palpable. Although probably only seconds, it seemed like time stood still before the four volunteers, acting as if of one mind, went over the side like a synchronous swim team. The Dolphin was brought back to the surface cradled in those eight arms.

For the next forty-eight hours, volunteers worked in two-hour shifts, keeping the Dolphin's blow hole above the water's surface. Along with the loss of severe bloating came a substantial increase in appetite. A good sign in any patient.

Gradually the Dolphin's strength began to return, along with its ability to float or submerge at will. The Dolphin was once again alone

in the pool, swimming with strong Dolphin-like movement patterns.

During the last week of my vacation, I visited the centre often and was happy to find the animal's respiration becoming clearer and deeper. By the time my friend and I left for home, the staff and volunteers were optimistic.

Although it's snowing as I look out my windows, today's mail brought sunny news. Photographs of a familiar Dolphin rejoining a wild pod in the Atlantic.

Threats to Marine Mammals

Young grey whale (ABOVE) dead on an Oregon beach. Hunpback whale (BELOW) Baja, California.

The exploitation of whales and seals has spread over the centuries from coastal to international waters.

Nowadays, marine mammals face a greater threat than ever before. The threat lies in the gross degradation of the environment and destruction of their life-support systems. Sources of concern for marine mammals' welfare are: pollution, interaction with fisheries, noise disturbance, habitat destruction, and global environmental changes.

Chemical compounds that do not break down and that travel through the food chain are the most threatening category of pollutants for marine predators. Each successive level in the food chain tends to receive a higher cumulative dose of pollution than the preceding one. This is why long-lived animals like marine mammals, which are exposed over a long time to pollution via their food, are more at risk of accumulating pollutants than short-lived ones.

Fisheries interactions negatively affect marine mammals in two main ways: by the incidental killing of animals unintentionally caught and killed by fisheries nets (bycatch) and by prey depletion.

The impact of prey depletion resulting from overfishing and poor fisheries management has already caused the collapse of some local fish populations worldwide.

Cetaceans (whales and dolphins) live in a world where the dominant sense they use to understand their environment is a refined sense of hearing. There are a variety of human-made noises that may have an impact on cetaceans. Seismic testing, used in the exploration for oil and gas, is one of the more powerful sources of noise pollution. Ship and boat traffic is also a major noise source and a new threat has recently arrived with the introduction of seal scammers (acoustic anti-predator devices) at some fish farms. Cetaceans may be driven away by noise and excluded from areas that are important to their survival.

Worldwide coastal areas in particular are under tremendous pressure from a range of activities that can physically alter marine habitats.

These include land-based activities such as deforestation and river diversion; mining and construction-related activities; energy production; and aqua-culture, notably the development of fish farms. Changes in the physical nature of the habitats may make them less suitable for marine mammals.

Perhaps the threat that the least is known about is posed by global changes to the atmosphere. Temperature has a profound effect on food stocks. Colder sectors of the oceans, notably areas of upwellings, are exceptionally productive. These areas are feeding grounds for many marine mammal species.

An example of the effect of water temperature on food is provided by the case of krill, tiny shrimp-like creatures which play a key role in the food chain of the greatest aggregation of whales in the world, located in the southern ocean. The extraordinary productivity of krill reflects a number of localised conditions, including the convergence of warm and cold currents in the southern oceans, leading to nutrient-rich upwellings around the shores of Antarctica.

Besides an increase in temperature, a number of other physical changes predicted for the ocean have the potential to drastically influence mammals, indeed all marine life. Such physical changes include global circulation patterns, shifts in the degree of salinity at different locations and changing pH levels (the measure of the acidity-alkalinity balance in water.)

Another possible change in ocean ecosystems could arise from the depletion of the ozone layer. It is well known that phytoplankton is susceptible to ultraviolet rays. If phytoplankton should decline in quantity and distribution due to increased UV radiation, there would probably be two pronounced repercussions. The first is that many marine food chains would lose their base nutrients and a ripple effect of starvation would pass through the animals dependent on krill, with all that implies for larger creatures at higher levels. The second involves the global carbon cycle. Oceans are thought to absorb about half of all carbon emitted into the global atmosphere each year. A vital role in this absorption is played by the photosynthetic activity of phytoplankton.

Stefania Gaspari

RUNNING WITH A KNIFE

I did a U-turn in the intersection, flipped on my emergency light, and sped toward the cove. On the way, I called the local marina and asked them to page a friend, telling him where to meet me and not to spare the horses getting there. There was no time to lose.

A local couple, sipping cocktails on their dock, had been enjoying the wildlife in their small harbor, especially one Seal who seemed to have taken up residence about 200 yards offshore.

They'd been watching it for the last two hours, but as the tide started coming in—and less and less of the animal was exposed above the waterline—it occurred to them their entertaining resident Seal was in trouble.

When I first got the call on my cell phone, a wave of panic rushed over me. It was my guess the couple had been leisurely watching a Seal—no doubt terrified—entangled in a discarded fishing net and fighting for its life. And nothing was surer; as the moon exerted its control on the tides, the animal would be unable to keep its head above water and would slowly drown.

Fortunately I had a wetsuit in the truck, although I hoped it wouldn't be necessary this time out. In animal rescue you can count on time spent standing or wading in frigid waters, so I'd learned to be prepared. A wetsuit was standard equipment.

As I drove the last mile, I called the couple for an update and asked if they'd seen a boat coming in their direction. They said yes, they had spotted the boat, but "Never mind coming," they added, because the ocean had just covered the animal.

I got this news as I skidded into their driveway. I don't even remember if I turned the engine off. I hit the gravel drive in a full sprint with the wetsuit under my arm and a large fishing knife in hand. (Yes, Mom, I was running with a knife.) As I ran down the dock, the rescue boat was just pulling up. The choreography was perfect. I jumped into the boat and demanded the couple tell me where the animal was. "But it's too late," they told me again.

"Just tell me where it is!" I ordered, fresh out of patience and time. Looking startled, they pointed off toward some branch-like debris protruding above the surface of the water. We took off.

Seals have evolved the ability to hold their breath for very long periods of time, up to half an hour, and even if unconscious from a traumatic blow, they won't fill their lungs with sea water. As far as I was concerned, this animal was still alive.

My plan was to drop the boat's winch line overboard, hook it to the entanglement, and crank it to the surface. If this worked, we could then take our time freeing the seal. This was Plan A.

We circled the debris. A rather weak swimmer, I didn't relish the

The middle sea lion is suffering from deep wounds inflicted by a fishing net.

thought of my coming plunge. I spit into my mask, wondering where Lloyd Bridges was when you needed him, took a deep breath, and made my first dive. Even through a wetsuit, the low water temperature was a shock.

Visibility was poor, but I could see enough to confirm the situation was exactly what I'd envisioned. Except for one thing. Our victim wasn't a Seal; it was a California Sea Lion—a big male. He was tangled in a section of discarded gill net, which in turn was snarled in a tree stump, its substantial root system still attached. The waterlogged stump rested solidly on the bottom. I swam around to the front of the animal. The sheer terror of his situation was etched on his face. His eyes looked like two 60-watt lightbulbs.

I kicked to the surface and yelled for the hook to be lowered. "I think the stump is too big," I said, "but let's give it a try."

I dove again, this time pulling a steel cable behind me. I wrapped the cable around a section of the stump and hooked the cable back to itself, then I surfaced and gave the thumbs up. My friend started to crank the hand winch, but as the cable strained, the back of the boat lowered into the water. It wasn't going to work.

I asked for the fishing knife and dove again.

It's a popular notion that wild animals in trouble instinctively know when we're trying to help them. Not true. At least not for this Sea Lion. When I swam toward him, his lips pulled back to expose four canine teeth threatening enough to star in a nightmare. And when I tugged on the net, he thrashed wildly in an effort to turn in my direction. Fortunately for both of us, his movements were limited by his prison of gill net.

I went up for a few breaths, not having made any cuts and knowing the next dive would be my last. When I went down this time, for safety's sake, I stayed behind the Sea Lion. Finally, I got the blade between the animal and the net. A few cuts with the knife and the Sea Lion rocketed to the surface. I was told later by my friend in the boat that he'd "exploded into the air." By the time I surfaced, he was swimming hard to the open

ocean. As for me, I was cold and tired, but I made one more dive to cut away and retrieve the net. There would be other ocean travelers dropping into this cove. No need for them to share the Sea Lion's fate.

MOUTH TO BEAK

In the darkened barn, the pungent odor of livestock assaulted my nose. It struck me again how different domesticated animals smell from those born to be wild. The result of diet? Perhaps. Or had I simply learned to smell a wild animal's fear, much like the predator they mistook me for would do?

As my pupils widened to take in more light, I spotted the object of my search, a Red-Tailed Hawk, grounded in a dusty, black corner. Wounded and wary, this Hawk watched my every move. And for several minutes I observed his.

It's important to get an idea as to what an animal's injuries are before capture and restraint. If the animal has a broken leg, you certainly don't want to grab that leg in your efforts to restrain it.

This bird's left wing tip was dragging on the ground. But I had to assume his taloned feet and that flesh-eating beak were in full working order. Wearing welding gauntlets to protect my hands, I approached carefully. The bird, cornered and terrified, puffed himself up to look as large and forbidding as possible. His beak was open and

he'd leaned back to fighting stance, prepared to counter my attack with readied talons. I've captured many birds of prey, and the experience has taught me to move quickly. In seconds I'd snatched the startled bird off the ground. I immediately placed him in a carrier and covered it with a towel to obscure his view.

At the Centre, I tube-fed the Hawk an electrolyte solution to help correct any fluid deficit, then left him to rest quietly in the dark carrier. A more thorough examination and X rays would come when he was in less stress.

The examination revealed a broken wing. The X ray told us the fracture was in the mid-shaft area of the left ulna (about halfway down the wing). The smaller radius bone was intact. (The ulna and radius are the two bones you feel in your own forearm.) The injury must have been very recent because, other than being a bit dehydrated, the Hawk was of good weight and muscle tone. The mid-shaft location of the fracture, the freshness of the break, and the bird's excellent health made him a viable candidate for surgical repair. Surgery to apply a kirchner-type splint to the fracture was scheduled for the following day.

First the bird was anaesthetized using isoflourine gas. My role in the surgery was to monitor the Hawk's respiration and make adjustments to the amount of anaesthetic he was inhaling. The area of the fracture was plucked of all feathers, thoroughly cleaned, and a small incision was made by the surgeon to expose the bone ends. A small

polypropylene rod or pin was inserted into one bone end, then pulled back halfway into the other bone end by a thin wire attached to the rod. Because long bones in birds do not contain marrow and are hollow, this type of procedure is possible. A special fast-drying glue was injected around the rod. This lightweight pin would become a permanent addition to the bird's anatomy.

Next, four stainless steel pins were forced through the bone and plastic rod. The four pins were placed perpendicular to the bone and in alignment with each other, like telephone poles down a road. This made up the structure for the external fixation device that added rigidity to the site and ensured perfect alignment was maintained.

While the surgeon did her job, I did mine, monitoring the Hawk's respiration. Everything was going well until . . .Yes, I was sure of it. "The bird's stopped breathing," I announced. Activity halted immediately, and the surgeon's eyes fixed on the small rib cage in front of us. "Well, that's it," she said, putting down her instruments. "He's gone." "I don't think so," I replied. I pulled the anaesthetic cone from the Hawk's head and placed my mouth over his face. Gently, I began to breathe air into the bird's lungs. Gently is the operative word here. Avian lung capacity is considerably less than my own.

Seeing I had no intention of letting the bird go without a fight, the surgeon shouted into the next room for a respiratory stimulant. A few drops were placed under the bird's tongue while I continued mouth-to-beak respiration. Periodically I stopped and watched as the

Hawk took a half dozen breaths on his own, then stopped again.

I couldn't help worrying, as I continued the exchange of oxygen from my lungs to the Hawk's, what would happen if the Red-Tail opened his eyes as I was lowering my open mouth over his face. My tongue was definitely in a vulnerable position. And there was his last meal—that rat I'd fed him twenty-four hours ago. But there was no going back now.

As I kept the Hawk alive, the surgeon worked at fast-forward speed. She sutured around the pins that protruded about one inch beyond the wing's surface, then pierced holes in a small piece of rubber tubing. The holes were aligned with the four pins and the tube was pressed down over the pins, close to the wing surface and parallel to the fractured bone.

After about fifteen minutes of breathing for the Hawk, its own respiratory rhythm kicked in. The vet completed the surgery by injecting a fast-drying epoxy glue inside the tube. The four pins and the glue-filled tube now fused into an inflexible unit.

We placed the Hawk, who was slowly regaining consciousness, on a heating pad in a dark, quiet cage for some well-needed rest.

The day after surgery, our Red-Tailed Hawk was alert and hungry, and we moved him to an outdoor enclosure called a mew. A mew gives Hawks privacy, plenty of fresh air and sunlight, and a safe view of the world. It has perches at varying heights, so a flightless bird can work its way to the level where it feels most comfortable. To ensure there would be as little loss of muscle tone and range of motion as possible, the Hawk's wing was neither bandaged nor wrapped to his body. This would also make it easier for the bird to maintain his balance.

Six weeks after surgery, the X rays revealed a strong union where there was once a fracture. It was time to remove the external splint.

This is not a surgical procedure, so I did it myself.

I administered a mild sedative, and with the bird conscious but unresponsive, and using heavy wire cutters, I cut all four metal pins between the wing surface and the epoxy-filled tubing. Using needle-nose pliers and a twisting, pulling motion, I removed each of the four stainless steel pins from the bone. The plastic pin was left inside the ulna to reinforce the bone at the site of the four small holes; later they would fill themselves in. Again, we left the bird to recover quietly on a heating pad. When he was well enough, we'd begin flight retraining, preparing him for release back to the wild.

In the final phase of the Hawk's rehabilitation we used a process known as creancing. The Red-Tail was fitted with leather anklets called jesses, which in turn were attached to a fishing line and reel. To afford more control, the reel was mounted on a short section of broom handle about twelve inches long. When the bird was secure, my colleague stood in the middle of an open field and tossed him into the air, allowing the bird to fly for about a hundred yards before bringing him down with a drag of her thumb on the reel. She kept this up as long as possible, careful to neither overstress nor tire the bird.

After weeks of this endurance training, the Hawk was flying strong and level with no sign of fatigue or open-mouthed breathing. The time had come for his second chance at life in the wild. We removed the anklets and once more threw the Hawk skyward. He soared high, and this time nothing pulled him back to earth.

HEART OF STEEL

Life in the wild is harsh and uncompromising. Books and documentaries depict the natural world as cruel, survival of the fittest being the caveat. But I believe that when it comes to cruelty, nothing can hold a candle to man and his hideous inventions.

The weather was mild and the snow that had fallen during the night lay undisturbed as I set out for a walk. So pristine was the landscape that my footsteps across the white blanket made me feel like a vandal. In reality, the only crime I was guilty of was trespassing; I was enjoying the meditative stillness of what I knew to be First Nations land. There were no people, no buildings, no utility poles, and no traffic noise. Months of stress were melting away from me like butter from a hot knife.

The animals I had lost this year, and those that had rallied, were not with me this afternoon as I walked along the river that swiftly flowed between narrow groves of cottonwood trees. My thoughts were of everything and of nothing, all at the same time. But as I rounded a particularly old, gnarled tree, I came across a sight that stopped me in my tracks.

Like a satanic snow angel, the Coyote's blood contrasted with the icy whiteness and burned into my retinas. I wanted to turn and run, to pretend this wasn't happening. But that's not what my life is about. I am devoted to giving aid to all wild animals. There is no such thing as a day off.

The Coyote's leg was severely mangled by the steel jaws of the leghold trap. I wanted to scream at the top of my lungs and voice my outrage and frustration to the world at this senseless brutality.

She was a female and she was in bad shape. The pain she endured was excruciating, but as I stepped closer to get a better look at the situation, the hair down her back stood erect and her lips curled back to expose her menacing canines, dripping with her own blood. Her threat display was so genuine and so raw that I was truly afraid to move. I forced my feet to retreat a couple of steps, and the struggling Coyote fell to her side.

It was then I saw her swollen mammaries. This Coyote had a cold, hungry litter somewhere, but the rusty jaws chewing through her leg had her chained to a tree.

"There must be something I can do," I heard myself say out loud. There was no doubt in my mind that I could not get close enough to free her leg, and merely unhooking the chain from the anchoring tree still left her in that horrific trap.

I headed for home at a jog interrupted by periods of walking. I'm not in bad shape, but running a couple of miles in the snow proved a challenge. While my legs didn't set any speed records, my mind raced. I had to get that trap off her leg without becoming a chew toy for a terrified Coyote myself. Under the circumstances, sedating her seemed a bad idea. She was too weak and cold, and besides, I needed her awake to show me where her den was. By the time I reached my place, I had a plan of sorts. I'd shield myself with a piece of plywood while I worked on the trap.

Plywood barriers, or herding boards, are commonly used when working with large marine mammals such as sea lions and elephant seals, so I already had a three-by-four board in my shop. I quickly cut a small semi-circle in the bottom edge so I could pin the Coyote's leg to the ground under it, then tossed the plywood and an animal carrier into my four-wheel drive and took off.

When I found her again, via a back road and after a trudge through a field, the helpless Coyote lay motionless. I thought she was dead. As I walked slowly closer, she dragged herself unsteadily to her feet. This time I didn't let her threat display turn me back. I walked towards her with the plywood barrier in front of me. As I crossed over into her domain, delineated by a bloody circle, she made a ferocious lunge towards me.

I heard her teeth crash against the wood as her full weight bounced off my shield and dropped to the ground. That was all the resistance she could muster. In her mind, life had just ended. I moved in and placed the notched plywood gently over her leg. She didn't move. With one hand pressing the top of the plywood, I held it in place between the Coyote and my too-vulnerable flesh.

I had seen these traps before, and I knew it would be difficult for me to open. I am not a very large person and it would take all my weight to counter the steel springs. Placing one foot on top of each side of the trap, and balancing with my hand on the plywood, I brought all my weight down on the trap. The springs compressed slightly but the jaws barely twitched. The second time, I bounced,

once again bringing all my weight down as hard as I could. The springs compressed and the rusty jaws fell open.

I raised the wood from her leg and she knew she was free. In an instant she got to her feet and hobbled away on three legs. Her hind leg swung freely as she made her way through the snow—it was barely still a part of her anatomy. As she disappeared into the woods I was a little disappointed that she never looked back. I was waiting for that one expression of gratitude that you would expect in a story like this.

I knew in this snow she'd be easy to follow, so I gave her a comfortable head start.

To disarm the trap, I threw a large stick into its gaping jaws, then watched in shock as it snapped the stick in two—as it had the Coyote's leg. I unwrapped the chain holding the trap to the tree, swung the trap a couple of times over my head, then let go and watched it sail out into the middle of the river. I exchanged the plywood for the carrier, hoisted it up on my shoulder, and set out to follow the mother Coyote's bloody trail through the snow.

I was amazed at how little deviation there was in her direction. She was going back to her pups and nothing was going to stop her. Her struggle, recorded in the snow, was heartbreaking. Every so often

it was apparent where she had fallen over, then pulled herself back to her feet and continued towards her pups. Each drop of life that flowed from her body led me closer to her babies. I found myself thinking of one of my favorite movies, *Eleni*, in which an innocent mother is facing a firing squad during the Greek Revolution. Just before the bullet silences her forever, she throws her arms into the air and screams, "MY CHILDREN!"

I followed the Coyote's trail into a clearing, dropped the carrier, and stopped to rest. The terrain changed here, becoming rocky before sloping up toward the foothills. It looked as if her trail ended somewhere in the rocks, so I decided to leave the carrier behind and have a look.

I moved with great caution. I doubted she had much strength left, but if she did and her pups were nearby, this is where she would make a stand.

It would make no difference to her that thirty minutes ago I was the one who removed the trap from her bloody leg.

I moved around a rock where the trail disappeared and climbed some slippery, snow-covered rocks to get a good vantage point. I was amazed at the view I suddenly had. There she was, lying in front of the opening to her den. I could see at least four tiny puppies. One was still suckling, one was climbing on mom, one had her tail in its mouth and was pulling, while the fourth was sniffing what used to be her leg. The pups seemed ecstatic to have her back.

Distracted for a moment by these beautiful little Coyotes, I hadn't noticed how still mom was. This was not merely the stillness of exhaustion or the stillness of sleep. The Coyote had struggled back to her children and died. A chill came over me as the realization of this drama began to sink in.

It was easy to gather up the terrified pups and drop them one by one into the airline kennel. There were six in all. We had a great secluded chain link enclosure where they could grow up wild and wary of humans.

In the months that followed their release back to the wild, the nights were filled with their mournful voices. Voices that I took great comfort in hearing.

Coyote Extermination

The coyote is an omnivorous animal that eats small rodents (especially mice and hares), animal carcasses, and several species of plants. Coyotes live in small groups and

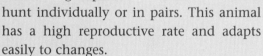

Until they can hunt on their own in the wild, pups nip at their mother's mouth until she regurgitates partially digested food to nourish them.

hunt individually or in pairs. This animal has a high reproductive rate and adapts easily to changes.

For most of this century, there has been hot debate in the western United States on the impact these animals have on livestock, particularly sheep. Sheep farmers, concerned that coyotes were eating their stock, wanted to see them exterminated. However, experts argued for the coyotes, pointing out that although coyotes were indeed killing and eating sheep, their presence was in fact beneficial for the entire ecosystem. The presence of coyotes is advantageous for the grazers because coyotes control the populations of small grazers—in particular hares—which compete with big herbivores such as sheep and cattle. A reduction in the coyote populations would lead to the disequilibrium of that particular ecosystem, and the farmers would then be faced with a plague of hares.

Up till now, the farmer's point of view predominated. Since 1940, farmers, together with the U.S. departments of the Interior and Agriculture, have waged a fierce battle against coyotes and wolves, predators for sheep and cattle respectively. Hunters and government employees killed a massive number of wolves through the Predator Control Program. This resulted in an increased population of coyotes because there were no wolves to prey on the coyotes, so the attempt to eradictae sheep predators was foiled.

From an ecological standpoint, it is also necessary to take into consideration the relationship between sheep, coyotes, and hares, and to balance the number of sheep killed by coyotes with the number of sheep which might have died if coyotes had not freed grazing ground from the encroachment of hares.

Many experts think that it would be less expensive for people to pay the farmers directly for every lost sheep or goat than to contribute millions of dollars each year for the Predator Control Program.

People have generally created more problems than they have solved by resorting to a strategy of extermination since the balance of nature is never as simple as it may appear.

Stefania Gaspari

JULIUS'S BIRTHDAY

There were no skid marks. According to the eyewitness report, the driver of the vehicle neither slowed down nor swerved, just drove off after the impact. The severely injured Doe had managed to drag herself out of the ditch and into the densest, most impenetrable thicket she could reach. While this was basic Deer instinct, too frequently it made my job much more difficult. I buttoned up my denim jacket, pulled on my cap, and donned work gloves and safety glasses. With a stethoscope around my neck and a syringe full of sedation in my pocket, I began the arduous crawl toward the accident victim. Blackberry thorns snagged my clothes and scratched my face as I worked my way deeper into the brush. There she was.

I could tell the Doe was aware of my presence by her ear movements and because, even though she was lying on her side, her legs were still trying to run. I approached from behind, respectful of her sharp hooves. My first concern was to relieve her stress so, arm extended, needle in hand, I injected the sedative into the thick muscle of her hind leg. Then I backed off and waited for the drug to take effect, about fifteen minutes.

While I cooled my heels in the thicket, an associate brought me a heavy blanket. I figured if I could clear enough space to spread it behind the Doe, I'd roll her onto it, and my colleague and I could drag her out. By breaking branches and shoving back the brush, I freed up enough area to work the blanket in behind her, then I reached over, grabbed her legs, and rolled her over.

I stared at her wide-eyed. I hadn't expected this. Her abdomen was greatly distended, and a few drops of colostrum-tinted milk oozed from her mammaries. Now, where there had been just one animal in jeopardy, there were two—and they'd both been sedated. We moved fast. Fortunately, now that the Doe was on the blanket, extricating her from the thicket was routine. Within half an hour we were back at the CentRE.

The Doe was gently placed on the grass in a small outdoor enclosure while I pondered the situation. I didn't exactly grow up on a farm, and I had never delivered anything, so I was a little confused as to how to proceed with this case. I started an intravenous flow of fluids into the Doe and went to make a phone call to a consulting veterinarian.

It was late afternoon before I reached her. I explained the Doe's circumstance and asked for some advice. "What do you think the Doe's chances are?" she asked.

"I think her chances are slim," I said. "It's the Fawn that concerns me."

She thought for a bit, then said, "You've got two ways to go. You can euthanize the Doe and take the Fawn now, or you can wait until the doe dies and get the fawn out within two minutes."

"What about the sedative?" I asked. "Will the Fawn start breathing on its own?"

"Good question . . . probably not," she said. "Just be ready to inject a stimulant."

I got off the phone, slightly shaken, and feeling a little bit alone. As I ran through the various ways of killing the Doe without endangering the unborn Fawn by the use of injectable euthanasia drugs, the idea of waiting looked better and better. Besides, what a way to come into the world.

We ran electricity out to the enclosure and set up quartz lights on tripods. We stocked up on clean towels and blankets and assembled a tray of supplies, including scalpels, a syringe of respiratory stimulant, a rubber nasal suction ball, plus a number of other items I couldn't possibly need. I gave the volunteers instructions and assigned everyone a two-hour Doe watch. As ready as I could be, I went back to my office to try and relax a bit and nibble at my fingernails.

I'd barely made it to my index finger when the door to my office burst open and a volunteer screamed, "She's dead!" I vaulted over my desk, my chair slamming into the wall behind me. We sprinted to the enclosure and I slid to the Doe on my knees while grabbing the razor-sharp scalpel. All eyes were fixed on the gleaming blade shaking in my hand. I took a deep breath, and made my first cut.

I didn't have a clear picture of exactly where, or in what position, the Fawn rested, but I knew I'd have to work my way through layers of tissue, and I'd have to be cautious. It would be a drag to get cut on your birthday. Keeping my hand as steady as I could, I continued to make long, shallow cuts. Then two more cuts, and the Fawn slid out and onto the blanket. For a second or two all any of us could do was stare.

Using the nasal suction ball, I set about clearing the fluid from the Fawn's throat and nose. There were no signs of respiration. The stethoscope magnified a soft heartbeat. Not hesitating now, I injected the stimulant. Still, no sign of respiration. Desperate, I placed my mouth over the fawn's tiny muzzle and gently exhaled. The Fawn's chest rose and dropped. I repeated the process, again and again and again.

Finally its own respiratory rhythm took over. Tears running down my cheeks, I passed the wet newborn to a waiting volunteer who wrapped it in a towel and rubbed it dry. The Fawn was a male, and we named him Julius. Julius was carried off to the treatment room for a warm bottle of formula and a chance to try out his rubbery legs. It would have been advantageous to mix some of the mother's colostrum with the formula, but I was concerned about the amount of sedative that might have been absorbed into the milk. Formula would have to do. And it seemed to be okay with Julius. Not knowing anything different, the orphan Fawn took quite naturally to the unnatural rubber nipple on a cola bottle.

Once we knew he had no feeding problems, we immediately put him in a warm, padded airline kennel. The next morning we introduced him to the other Fawns in the outdoor pen.

Endearing as he was, to ensure him a good chance for survival after his release, we cut off human contact as soon as possible. A Deer that survives is a deer that runs from human interaction. From the time he joined the other Fawns, Julius was observed in total silence through a hole in the fence surrounding the enclosure, and fed through a bottle rack built into the wooden fence. (We slip the bottles through the fence, leaving the nipples protruding on the other side at a level the  Fawns can easily reach.) Julius was greeted curiously but warmly by the four other residents of the deer pen. It is here that he will hopefully grow up healthy, strong, and wild.

DOE IN A HOLE

Wild animals have a true instinct for survival, but even the most adaptable of them cannot flourish in the face of constant technological intervention and human presence. They possess no knowledge of the dangers created by bulldozers, backhoes, and line-stringing utility companies. Construction sites, particularly those in previously wild areas, always pose a serious threat to many species.

A new home was under construction on the edge of the woods. Trees were being thinned, deep foundations were being excavated, and vast expanses of glass were in the offing. A large hole, maybe eight feet deep and ten feet wide, had been dug for a septic tank. A large concrete cube had been lowered into the hole, leaving a space of perhaps two feet between it and the soil on all four sides. The crew working on the project was fast, efficient, and thoughtless.

Five o'clock came and everyone went home for the weekend, leaving a gaping wound in the earth where just the night before was solid ground.

Later that same evening, a foraging Columbia Black-Tailed Doe fell to the bottom of the pit. The path she had walked and run a thousand times simply swallowed her whole. Concrete scraped her right side, cold damp earth chilled her left. She could barely move. Throughout the night she fought, kicking and twisting, struggling against her tomb, until she could struggle no more. Had she the energy to lift her head, she would have seen the moon and stars, but her battle for survival had drained her. Her world was darkness.

A man walking his dog happened on her the next morning and called the Wildlife Centre, leaving a cryptic message on our machine about a Deer and a hole.

Two of us went to investigate. Stepping out onto the concrete tank, I looked down on the Doe. She appeared exhausted. She had to be panicked by the close proximity of humans, but she didn't—or more likely couldn't—even lift her head.

The dirt wall in front of her bore the scarred record of her desperate but futile attempts to kick her way to safety. Either prior to her fall or during the night, water had seeped into the hole, leaving her standing in over three feet of icy, brackish water. Her forehead was rubbed raw and her swollen eyes were caked with mud. She didn't have much life left. We had to get her out—and quickly.

My assistant, Shawn, and I took a few minutes to brainstorm and come up with a plan. We decided we needed two things: more bodies to help, and some long, wide belts or straps. The idea was to work two sets of straps underneath the animal and, with people on both sides, hoist her out. I called the Center.

Within half an hour, help arrived, and we'd fashioned straps from rolled-up blankets, using rope to tie them tightly at each end. The next step was to sedate the Doe. Lying on my stomach on the concrete tank, I reached into the hole and administered an injection into her hip. I didn't foresee what happened next. The exhausted Doe's legs gave out and she collapsed below the water. Shawn didn't hesitate. He leaped into the pit and, standing chest deep in mud and frigid water, lifted and held the Doe's head above the surface. We quickly looped rope under her chin to hold her head up so Shawn would be free to work the makeshift belts under the Doe and pass the rope ends up to us. We positioned one belt under her abdomen and one under her ribcage. Each belt was held in a firm grip by two people at the surface, one to the left of the Doe and one to her right.

I instructed everyone to pull smoothly and quickly on the count of three. When a plan works it's a thing of beauty. The hapless Doe rose out of the hole as if a giant hand had reached down and picked her up.

We started intravenous fluids flowing into her body through a vein in her leg and loaded her into the back of the pickup for trans-

port to the Centre. Once there we laid her in a quiet field. As she slept we cleaned her wounds, rinsed the debris from her eyes, then administered a homeopathic eye lotion consisting of Calendula (marigold), Euphrasia (eyebright), and sterile water. Calendula is a potent healing agent, while the Euphrasia soothes the eye and relieves pain. Together they're a very effective eye remedy. When

we'd removed the IV, we quietly walked away, leaving her to sleep off her nightmare experience. She was a lucky Doe, and we hoped, with a little more luck, she'd wake and wander back to her woodland home. Two hours later there was only her impression left in the tall grass.

On Monday we did two things: made the construction company aware of the results of its carelessness, and shopped for wide rescue straps to add to our equipment.

The next time we had a Doe in a hole—and, sadly, we fully expected there would be a next time—we'd be ready.

OWLS

Most of the animals that find themselves in a rehabilitation facility are birds. Of the hundreds of birds we are faced with, the different species of Owls can be the most fascinating. Although there are many qualities that Owls have in common, they vary greatly in size, appearance, and diet. I have worked with the tiny Flammulated Owl, just six inches tall, which feeds on moths and other insects. At the other end of the scale, I've had experiences with Great Horned Owls, which can be two feet tall and are the scourge of the night-time skies, feeding on mammals and birds of all sizes and description. A Great Horned Owl will even kill skunks and porcupines and can routinely kill birds as large as Canada geese and swans. There is no denying that this Owl is a fierce predator.

Generally speaking, Owls are a real pleasure to work with. They have a very calm demeanor and seem to adjust well to their brief captivity. Many types of birds are so highly strung and so panicked by the sight and sound of humans that it is not unusual for them to compound the seriousness of their initial injuries by repeatedly flying into the sides of their enclosures. Owls, on the other hand, have a tendency to sit quietly and glare.

The first Owls we received this season were two nestling Great Horned Owls. Nothing more than a palmfull of down, these two babies fell to earth from a great height when the tree that held their nest was cut down for profit. Our most immediate concern was to find out if they had sustained any serious injuries from the fall. They appeared to be in good shape, but only time would tell for certain.

We were fortunate that they were admitted as a pair. A lone baby of any species creates a host of new problems. Animals must be raised in the company of what we call a *conspecific*. In other words, a Great Horned Owl must grow up looking at and interacting with another Great Horned Owl. For birds of prey such as Owls, there is a brief period of time, when they are around two to three weeks old, when the bird establishes its social imprinting or species identification. If the nestling Owl is sharing a space with a conspecific, it will grow up with the proper self-image, so to speak. If the nestling is being hand-fed by humans and has no other Owl present, its social imprinting will be that of a human. If it is later released, this misimprinted Owl will not identify with its own species. It will have no understanding of territoriality. And when it reaches sexual maturity, it will seek out a human.

Once it identifies its potential mate, it will then start attacking other people in the area to chase them out of its territory and away from its mate.

You may have seen photographs of Bald Eagles and Peregrine Falcon chicks being fed with hand puppets made to look like their parents. This is so they may be safely hand-raised by humans who are trying to reintroduce the species to the wild and ensuring they learn their proper social orientation. At the Centre, we will either try to borrow an animal from another centre to keep ours company, or we will transfer our animal to a facility already housing conspecifics. If we are confident the animal is beyond the age of imprinting, it can safely be housed and rehabilitated by itself.

With Owls, it is usually not too difficult to know if they have imprinted on their own species. Owls have very pronounced posturing and threat displays when confronted by an alien species. In a few weeks, when I walked into the enclosure housing our two young Great Horned Owls, there was very loud beak clacking, extended wings with head bobbing, and if I didn't get the message, they would try to part my hair with their talons, frequently drawing blood.

I have gone into some detail about social imprinting because it is an extremely critical subject to both the rehabilitator and the individual who may find a baby animal. All too often, a well-intentioned family finds a baby Owl or Hawk that has fallen from a nest. It seems like it will make a great family project and be an educational experience for the kids. After several critical weeks of hand-feeding the bird (usually the wrong diet), the family brings the bird into the rehabilitation centre. What on the surface appears to be a success story is in reality a tragedy. A bird of prey imprinted on humans cannot be released back to the wild. The only remaining options are a life in captivity or, sadly, euthanasia. Please, if you find a baby animal in need, do what's best for the animal. Don't keep it. Don't feed it. Seek professional care.

Our nestling Owls were fed a steady diet of mice and small rats. For the first couple of days, they were given only small bits of meat, with no fur or bone. Once we were sure the Owlets were digesting the meat properly, small bits of bone and fur were added to the diet. The fur and bone are critical sources of roughage and calcium. Eventually these Owls were swallowing mice whole and tearing apart rats on their own. As they began to lose their down and show some mature plumage and an interest in exercising their wings, they were moved to a small flight cage.

During the following weeks, as our young Great Horned Owls grew to be fierce hunters, many other Owls came and went at the centre. Two Northern Saw-Whet Owls came in with head traumas. Saw-Whets are tiny owls with large, sweet faces. They are frequently struck by automobiles while they are feeding around the short grass along highways. These two were lucky. After a week of fluids, homeopathic Arnica for the physical trauma, and a good mouse diet, they were on their way.

One patient that was not so lucky was an adult Great Horned Owl that was blown out of a tree by some moron with a shotgun. I still have trouble imagining what sort of person derives enjoyment from taking another life. The Owl had a badly shattered wing and numerous pellets throughout its body. Our veterinary surgeon tried to repair the damage, but the Owl died during the long procedure.

Probably the most unique looking Owls to cross our threshold are the Barn Owls. They have a large, white, heart-shaped facial disc. I think they look a bit like flying monkeys. If you have Barn Owls

around your property, you need not worry about a rodent problem. Barn Owls are voracious hunters that swoop down on their prey on perfectly silent wings. These new arrivals were three nestlings that had apparently been orphaned, oddly enough, in a barn. They were uninjured and in good condition. Rehabilitating them would be routine.

Not only are Barn Owls unique in appearance, but they also have vocalizations that are hard to forget. As you approach a Barn Owl, you are greeted with a long, threatening hiss. Move in closer and that hiss graduates to a banshee-like scream. Judging from the sound, an onlooker would be certain you were causing the owl great bodily harm. Along with the vocalizations come some pretty interesting threat displays. The wings are outstretched and the Owl lowers its head and shakes it slowly from side to side. This is referred to as "toe dusting." If none of this deters your approach, the Barn Owl will not hesitate to launch its talons into your face. If you must get this close, it's a good idea to extend a gloved hand out in front.

As we prepared the Barn Owls for their return to the wild, the young Great Horned Owls were also getting close to being released. There was still one important lesson for them to master: they must learn to kill. This is an aspect of the rehabilitation process that many volunteers and visitors would rather not know about, but if young Owls do not learn to kill their own prey before being released, there is a strong possibility they will not survive.

A large portion of the owl flight cage is covered with thick leaf litter. This gives the small rodents a place to hide and simulates a realistic hunting situation. Great Horned Owls are capable of successfully finding and striking their prey with only their ears to guide them. Owls that specialize in night hunting have amazing anatomical adaptations. The large dish-like face or facial disc actually catches sound and focuses it back toward the ear openings. The placement of the ears is also quite special. Located on either side of the outer edge of the disc, one ear is slightly higher than the other. By moving its head from side to side and up and down, the Owl is able to pinpoint the exact location of the rustling.

The quickest way for Owls to learn hunting techniques is by example, so we housed the youngsters with an older experienced hunter and withheld a couple of feedings. A hungry owl is much more apt to make a first kill than a fat satisfied owl. Once they showed their abilities as hunters, our young Great Horned Owls were ready for freedom.

Owl releases are generally not too dramatic. We just leave the door to the flight open as evening approaches. When the Owls decide to leave, they leave. Sometimes we continue to place food in the flight cage for a few days. If an owl is not a successful hunter immediately, it may return for an easy meal. More often than not, we never see them again.

On the surface, Owl rehabilitation may seem mundane. Rescues are rarely exciting. Releases are anything but Kodak moments. However, if you are a patient person with an eye for detail and subtleties, a visit from any Owl species is fascinating.

SLOTHS, CROCS, AND PRIMATES

Even in the shade, the Costa Rican climate was killing me. From the moment I stepped off the airplane, I felt as if some alien force had locked on a tractor-beam and was draining my energy. The bus ride to the edge of the rain forest left me soaking wet and about five pounds shy of my former self. "How can anyone live in the tropics?" I thought to myself.

Back home it was winter, and a slow time for a rehabilitation centre. It seemed like a good opportunity to get away and experience some exotic species. The jeep from the wildlife preserve, driven by Ernesto, the facility director, was waiting for me by the side of the road. The light filtering in through the forest canopy was tinted green by the time it reached us. Periodically the jeep would stop. As my ears adjusted to the stillness, it became apparent that the forest was any-thing but silent. There was a symphony of calls coming from every level under the thick canopy. I didn't even know if I was hearing birds or monkeys, but the sounds penetrated deeply into my nervous system. It may have been the oppressive heat and humidity or sensory overload, but that was the closest I had ever come to being hypnotized.

The sound of the old four-cylinder engine grinding to a start brought me back once again, and we continued on. Over the din of the engine, Ernesto talked about the threats to wildlife in the area. As in most of the world, loss of habitat topped the list.

Millions of acres of rain forest are being destroyed for short-term agriculture, logging, and livestock grazing. In the rain forest, most of the nutrients are in the vegetation itself. Topsoil doesn't really exist in the jungle. When rain forest land is cleared and burned, it can only support agriculture for a few years before the farmer must move to new land—gained by razing even more rain forest—creating a vicious cycle in which neither people nor wildlife win.

Not only is the rain forest the source of one-third of the earth's oxygen and one-fourth of all fresh water on our planet, it is also the home of countless species of wildlife. When millions of acres are devastated by slashing and burning, some of these species simply cease to exist. Others, to sustain themselves, crowd into neighboring areas where food sources are already stretched thin by the resident animal population. For the most part, the animals die right along with the forest.

Quick profits from the illegal pet trade also take a heavy toll on many Costa Rican species.

When we came to a clearing, Ernesto pointed off in the distance and what previously looked like solid jungle took on some human-made qualities. Buildings and animal enclosures began to distinguish

themselves from the trees and vines. Overhead walkways appeared as shortcuts between dense areas. The wildlife refuge had the look of something out of the *Swiss Family Robinson*. The structures were romantic and rustic, hand-built funky and substantial at the same time. It seemed as if the forest and the structures were locked in a constant struggle to dominate. Or rather, the forest was dominating and the facility was just trying to hold its own. My first impression of this refuge stirred such deep feelings within me that, had it not been for my intolerance of the climate, I am certain I would not have left.

After brief introductions to some of the staff and volunteers, most of whom spoke English as poorly as I spoke Spanish, we set out on a tour of the facility. Our first stop was a cage of confiscated Scarlet Macaws. I'd seen these brilliantly colored birds before—one or two at a time—but the impact of forty or fifty in a medium-sized flight cage was stunning, like a front-row seat at a fireworks display. I could have pulled up a chair and watched them for hours, but we were interrupted by an urgent message from one of the volunteers.

The only word I could make out was Cocodrilo, but whatever was

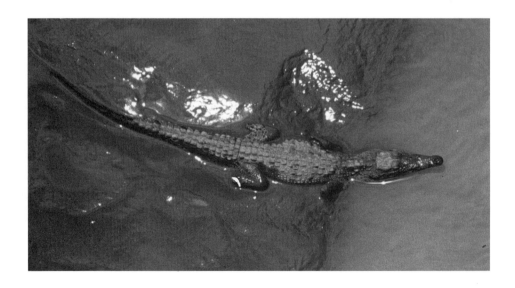

said put Ernesto and me back in the jeep, followed closely by a beater of a pickup carrying four more volunteers. "A routine animal relocation," I was told. A small Crocodile had been spotted in a shallow drainage area too close to an inhabited area. Our job was to capture the animal and move it a safe distance away.

We stopped at the edge of a village located near a foul-smelling swamp. The water was shallow, leaving the Crocodile plainly visible. The reptile was easily ten to twelve feet long. While motioning me to stay put, the five men moved off to surround the creature, wading fearlessly into the murky water. One man carried a long pole with a rope noose on the end, one man had a plain pole, and a third had another rope. The other two had just the hats on their heads. No one spoke.

When the Croc fixed his attention on the man directly in front of him, the man in the rear position poked him with a stick to create a diversion. The critical player in this action was the man on flank. Slowly he extended the pole with the noose on the end, then suddenly looped the noose over the animal's long snout, temporarily locking its jaws shut. Once the noose was in place, the other men converged on the thrashing reptile. The surface of the swampy pool erupted and the men went into fast-forward motion, with poles and rope ends flying in all directions. In the turmoil I couldn't figure out who was winning, the Crocodile or his well-meaning captors. In seconds it was over; the Croc was immobilized. When the men carried him out of the swamp, he looked like something that makes animal lovers everywhere cringe: an enormous piece of very expensive luggage. But this animal wasn't destined for an airport carousel. His destination was a Crocodile-friendly river a safer distance from encroaching civilization.

Back at the refuge, a gun-shot victim waited. In this instance I could at least lend some assistance.

The unfortunate patient was an animal I'd been anxious to see in the flesh, although not in this sorry condition. Lying helplessly on the table in front of me, its fur matted with its own blood, was a Three-Toed Sloth.

We cleaned the wound on this docile animal thoroughly. The injuries did not seem too extensive. The bullet went completely through the thigh, cleanly missing the bone. The refuge currently had no antibiotics available, but I was packing my homeopathic emergency kit. I administered remedies for shock and possible infection, and the Sloth was put away in a quiet cage filled with native flora.

To prepare for my Costa Rican adventure, I had done quite a bit of preparatory reading about the local animals. The Sloth, a seemingly lackluster animal, is really quite intriguing. Sloths live in the upper levels of the forest canopy and watching one move through a tree is akin to watching the minute hand on a clock. A Sloth has an incredibly slow metabolism and a ruminant-like stomach that allows it to digest the foliage that makes up its diet. Once a week the Sloth makes its way down from the treetops to defecate and urinate on the forest floor, push a little dirt and leaves over the waste, then slowly make its way back up the tree. Scientists do not know exactly why the Sloth is driven once a week to expose itself to so many predators on the forest floor, but the forces are strong.

Perhaps most fascinating of all is a life cycle that continues on a much more subtle level. The Sloth Moth, or Pyralid Moth, is found only in the thick fur of the Sloth. When the Sloth descends to the floor, the Moth hops off and lays her eggs on the dung, then returns to the Sloth for the trip back into the canopy.

With the Sloth doing well, and a lull in the daily chores, we toured the rest of the facility, stopping first at a large enclosure alive with tiny primates so lively and active you'd swear they were raised on pure caffeine.

They were confiscated Squirrel Monkeys, a popular but illegal pet. The members of this large group, too long and too closely associated with humans, would never see their wild home again. They had long since lost their ability to survive without human interference.

One of the animals had an eye infection and I suggested I treat it with some eyedrops I had in my kit. We entered the enclosure through a double safety door designed to prevent any of the animals from escaping.

It was easy to see why these little guys would spend their life in captivity. As soon as we passed through the second doorway, we were covered in Monkeys. They were on our shoulders, in our hair, up our legs, and in our pockets. When we singled out our target Monkey and I produced the dropper bottle, every Monkey in the enclosure grabbed for it. Eventually we placed a couple of drops in our patient's eye—and a couple in its mouth, some on its head, and a little more down its back—but we were successful. After peeling all the Monkeys from our bodies we escaped through the double door as they all went to examine their damp friend.

A volunteer and two German tourists who'd come to report an injured bird were waiting for us in the main building. The tourists seemed knowledgeable about wildlife and identified the bird as a Harpy Eagle. It was downed, they said, in a cultivated field not too far from the refuge. When they'd given us detailed directions as to the location, we jumped back in the jeep. On the way, Ernesto admitted having no eagle experience and said he was counting on my expertise.

At the thought of working with the Harpy, both my imagination and my adrenaline raced. The Harpy Eagle is the fiercest, most powerful winged predator on the planet. A crested giant measuring up to forty inches from beak to tail, it stands on legs that are two inches thick. Having no knowledge of its temperament or behavior when approached, I grew somewhat anxious as we neared our destination.

Turning down roads and paths that scarcely seemed passable, Ernesto knew where he was going, and before long we stopped on the edge of a manioc field. We grabbed a couple of blankets and some gloves and started across the field. (The blankets weren't thick, and in truth, knowing the Harpy, the only blankets I would have been comfortable with were the padded ones used by moving companies.) Ernesto stopped abruptly and pointed to the left. The brush was alive with movement. Slowly we walked toward it.

I spotted the bird through the vegetation. I could see its large black crest standing erect on top of its head. Heart pounding, I slipped my hands into the flimsy protective gloves and took a firm grip on my blanket.

Perspiration trickled down my rib cage. Within ten yards I got my first good look at the injured bird. I stared in disbelief. It was huge all right, but not at all threatening and nothing like I expected. Ernesto laughed.

"What's so funny?" I asked.

"*Crax rubra*," he said, still laughing.

"*Crax rubra, Crax rubra*," I repeated, dredging up my Latin. Then it came. *Crax rubra*. The great Curassow.

I'd been sweating bullets over the Costa Rican equivalent of a turkey. With the exception of the crested head, a Curassow has as much in common with the fierce Harpy Eagle as a pigeon has with a peregrine. A mostly terrestrial bird, the Curassow is now threatened by loss of habitat. (The fact it's also delicious when roasted hasn't helped its waning numbers.)

Both relieved and disappointed that I wasn't pitted against a Harpy, I gently trapped the Curassow under my blanket and bundled him off to the jeep. The bird was black with a rounded crest and a yellow knob at the base of the upper beak. The yellow knob and over-all black color identified him as male.

His injury? A fractured radius. The Curassow is a ground feeder, so the wing injury wouldn't hinder his ability to feed, but it could prove fatal if he encountered a predator and needed to take flight. To encourage proper healing of the fracture, I applied a figure-eight bandage to immobilize the wing. In about six weeks he would be in good shape.

My first day of helping these exotic species came to an end as a magnificent tropical thunderstorm engulfed the refuge. That night, as I tried to fall asleep on damp sheets, my mind was filled with anticipation of the animals that might cross my path tomorrow.

Diversity: The Key to Life

The fundamental levels of biological organization are genes, species, and ecosystems.

Genetic diversity refers to the genetic differences between individuals within a species. Species diversity refers to the different animals and plants that have evolved and adapted to exist in specific habitats. Ecosystem diversity refers to the different habitats on earth—lakes, deserts, oceans, temperate forests or tropical jungles, etc. The diverse environmental conditions of our planet have determined the way in which organisms and ecosystems have evolved and is responsible for the diversity of life around us.

Every species stores genetic information that is the result of millions of years of evolution and adaptation to variable environmental conditions. The rise and extinction of species regulates the biological diversity. Maintaining the genetic variability of species will ensure the evolution of life.

About 95 percent of the animals that have lived on earth are now extinct, so why is there all the fuss about species extinction? The concern is due to the rate

In an area where environmental groups have exposed the natural devastation caused by overharvesting, many westcoast forest companies finally seem willing to listen.

at which species are now being extinguished. The principal cause of biodiversity loss is habitat destruction that inevitably results from the expansion of human population and activities. In addition to habitat destruction, other direct causes are hunting, collection, and persecution.

Virtually all forms of human activity result in the modification of natural habitats which alters the abundance of species and in some cases leads to their extinction. Natural habitats are replaced by houses, hotels, highways, etc. This leads to habitat fragmentation and can potentially divide a population into smaller sub-populations. If a sub-population is too small, it is likely to become extinct in a short time. Populations that are reduced to low numbers may be forced to inbreed, as closely related individuals mate. This leads to a loss of genetic variation.

People ask, "Why should we bother to conserve wild species?" Conservation is important because the loss of just a few populations can result in a great destabilization of natural ecological communities. For example, pollination by birds and insects is essential for much plant (and, therefore, food) cultivation.

If we consider the environment as a marketable good, there are many reasons why we should conserve wild species. For one thing, they are economically important; for instance they have a medical importance. Almost half of the medical remedies used worldwide contain extracts of wild species of plants. Wild species of plants and animals have a scientific value, helping scientists to understand how life evolved on our planet and how it will continue to evolve.

For many people, animals and plants represent a focus for recreational activities like hunting, fishing, and photography. Ecotourism yields close to US$30 billion per year around the world. For example, wild animals such as lions and elephants draw tourists to African countries for activities such as big game and photographic safaris. This tourism is an important source of income for those countries.

By conserving wild species we will preserve a biological resource and maintain the biosphere for the support of the planet and human life.

Stefania Gaspari

RESURRECTION

I don't usually respond to dead animal calls, but this was a Deer, and our birds of prey needed fresh meat. As it was late afternoon New Year's Eve and I wasn't otherwise occupied, I decided to take the call and act as butcher for a good cause.

Apparently a Deer misjudged the height of a barbed wire fence, caught its hind legs, and hung itself up in the fence until it froze to death. I scribbled some directions on a note pad, grabbed a first aid kit with wire cutters, stuffed a stethoscope in my pocket, and set out.

My search took me along a rural road until, across a wide pasture, I spotted the Deer. I trudged over the snow-covered field and as I drew nearer, the scene turned uglier. The Deer, hanging upside down about three feet off the ground, had all four feet tangled in barbed wire. Her struggle must have been monumental. Beneath her, the freshly fallen snow was an abstract in blood. I started on the wire and it cut easily, the strands leaping away from the snapping jaws of the tool. With the last cut, the carcass crashed to the ground like a hundred-pound sack of dog food. I continued cutting until there was an opening large enough for me to drag the body through, then checked for a heartbeat with my stethoscope. Nothing. That was it then, fresh venison tonight.

I crammed my stethoscope back in my pocket and took hold of the Deer's hind legs in preparation for the haul across the field, but as I started to pull her, I noticed—or thought I noticed—the slightest movement in her throat. Had she just swallowed?

No. Not possible, I thought.

Then I remembered an old episode of *M.A.S.H.* in which a comatose soldier is mistaken for dead until a lone tear trickles down his cheek as he's given the last rites. My plans changed instantly.

I ran to the truck and retrieved a blanket and the first aid kit. When I got back to the Deer, I crushed a homeopathic remedy and placed it inside her lip. (I used Carbo Veg, vegetable charcoal, effective when there is imperceptible pulse, physical collapse, and the patient seems too weak to hold out.) Then I rolled her onto the blanket and, doing my best imitation of a sled dog, mushed back to the truck, pulling my frozen passenger behind me. With the Deer safely loaded, I stuck the flashing warning light on the roof and fish-tailed down the icy road as fast as I could while main-taining control

Because it was New Year's Eve, the Wildlife Centre was deserted, so I couldn't muster any help. I parked close to the door. Then, as gently as I could, I lowered the Deer, still on the blanket, to the ground. That accomplished, I dragged her through the reception area to the treatment room.

Once there I quickly plugged in several heating pads and rolled the Deer onto them, then placed hot water bottles all over her torso and covered her with more blankets. But when I removed the thermometer from the Deer's rectum, the mercury didn't register.

Maybe I was imagining things. Maybe she hadn't swallowed.

I warmed a litre of fluids to 100°F and began subcutaneous fluid therapy, injecting warm, sterile fluids under the animal's skin. This procedure causes large lumps to form at each injection site, but they soon disappear as the fluid is absorbed by the dehydrated tissue. The heating pads were set to low, to avoid burns, so now, other than keeping hot water bottles full, there was nothing to do but wait.

A few hours later her temperature finally registered 93.4°F, and I immediately turned my attention to cleaning and bandaging her wounds. Barbed wire is savage, and some of the lacerations on her legs were deep enough to expose bone. Her legs were still icy cold, but this didn't trouble me too much as the idea was to concentrate the heat on her torso in order to raise core temperature. In time, her circulation would return and her extremities would warm. I continued with the subcutaneous fluids, and her temperature rose to 96.6°F. At nine o'clock it was 98.2°F. Her wounds were beginning to bleed for the first time since I arrived on the scene. By ten o'clock her temperature leveled off at 100°F. I removed the heating pads and hot water bottles and left her covered with blankets. I decided to get some rest.

As an optimistic gesture, I hung blankets over the windows of the treatment room. If she was on her feet at first light, there was a good chance she would crash through a window to escape. I went upstairs to the apartment over the treatment room to get some sleep.

A little before midnight, I woke to the sound of kicking and banging from below. I lay there for a time, imagining the doe regain-

ing consciousness. Sometime later I got up and crept down the stairs to the dark, and now silent, treatment room.

I caught her in the beam of my flashlight. On the floor exactly where I left her. Just minutes before a new year was to begin—for me at least. My patient was dead.

I tried to find something positive in the day's events as I walked back to bed, but sometimes you just can't.

A SHOOT'N KIND OF GUY

Frank was a hunt'n, fish'n, shoot'n kind of guy. A real monosyllabic man's man. Frank's home was his castle, and when Frank got home from work, dinner was hot and the beer was cold. This night, however, was different. Frank's wife and two young daughters were waiting anxiously for him to get home so he could investigate the strange noises coming from above the kitchen ceiling. They'd heard them all day. There was something alive in the attic.

With all three of them talking at once, it took a minute for Frank to grasp the situation. It generally took Frank a minute to grasp any situation. Without wasting any time, he puffed up his chest, popped a beer, grabbed a flashlight, and strapped on his pistol. The trapdoor in the ceiling groaned resistance as Frank pulled the rope to unfold the ladder to the attic. Flashlight in one hand, beer in the other, Frank climbed the ladder with the resolve of a marine taking a hill.

When his head rose above floor level, he arced the flashlight to scan the whole attic. Everything appeared to be in its usual order. Or should I say disorder—it was, after all, an attic. After moving boxes marked "Playboy Mags" and old baby furniture covered in dust, Frank shone his light into the black corners, exposing only frightened spiders and mouse turds. But as he turned toward the only section left to inspect, a deep low growl came rolling out from behind a pile of paint-splattered drop cloths. Frank swung his light, locking it on two eyes glaring defiantly through a black mask.

She stood tall on her hind legs and growled a sincere warning. In a singularly stupid act, Frank went for his gun. Contained by the attic, the report shuddered through the house.

The mother Raccoon fell dead on top of her six traumatized babies.

"Come and get these things before I drown 'em," was the call I received. I hesitated before ringing the doorbell. I wasn't looking forward to this interaction. Self-control is not one of my strong suits. I'd just get in, I told myself, get the babies, and get out. No conversation. Trying to get people like Frank to look at the world from a different perspective is futile.

The tension in the family was oppressive. Clearly Frank was no one's hero tonight. I climbed the attic ladder, lifted the cold, dead mother off her babies, and placed them in the padded box I brought along. No one spoke as I left.

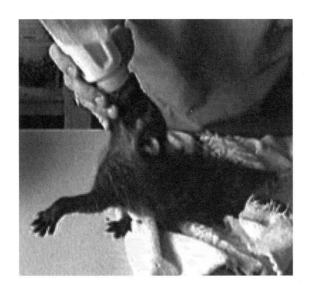

Humans acting as surrogate parents for wild Raccoons are always a second-rate substitute for the natural mom. There are things a human can do well enough, such as seeing to nutritional needs by bottle feeding with a milk replacement up to six times per day, watching the little stomachs fill up like balloons while being careful not to overfeed, and making sure they don't drink too fast, aspirate, and draw formula into their lungs. A human parent can even manage some toilet training, which entails tickling the kit's genital area with a damp cotton ball until it learns to urinate and defecate on its own.

But what of the things only a mother Raccoon can properly teach her young: recognition of food sources, foraging techniques, hunting and killing small prey, predator awareness? While some of these activities are instinctive, most are learned best by hanging out with mom. As surrogates we couldn't do it all, but we could do our best to compensate for the unnatural aspects of the rehabilitation process.

Fortunately, the six kits, each smaller than a handful and with eyes not yet open, were all in good health. The fact they wouldn't spend any time as starving orphans was also an advantage. It didn't take long for the litter to get used to the tiny latex nipples that brought them warm formula—except for the smallest kit. It seems there's always one in a litter, a runt, that is not only weaker, but also slower to adjust to the rehabilitation process. In the wild the runt might not survive, but at the Centre it quickly became everyone's favorite and got much special attention.

At about three weeks old, the young Raccoons' eyes opened and they got their first look at each other, their human parents, and the bizarre surroundings that made up their world so far. At four weeks, it was time to start introducing some solid food into their diets. Good-quality dog kibble provides balanced nutrition, and the first step was to soak the kibble and mix it with the formula in the bottles. Over the course of a few days, the Raccoons' digestive systems adjusted to this new food.

The time soon came for their first meal not presented in a baby bottle, a sort of kibble soup and formula mush we prepared in a shallow dish. They weren't impressed. I could almost hear them asking, "Where's our bottles?" We held their front legs back and repeatedly stuck their sassy faces into the mush. They were quick studies. Before long, all six kits were licking at the mush, falling in the mush, and wearing the mush. It was a regular free-for-all.

At around nine weeks old, the kits were living in an outdoor enclosure. Every few days we added something new to their diet: mice, worms, crayfish, and fruit. The only thing we avoided was table scraps, although they'd probably learn soon enough about the gourmet delights contained in garbage cans.

Finally, the juvenile Raccoons were moved to a larger, more isolated enclosure containing trees and logs, rocks and grass, and some running water. At this point we all but eliminated human contact. Any interaction we did have was intentionally loud, aggressive, and frightening to the Raccoons. We wanted the sight of humans to make them run for their hiding places, not conjure up cozy images of food and comfort.

The Raccoons thrived, growing fat, healthy, and athletic. They were also afraid of people and recognized myriad indigenous foods. It was time to plan their release.

We kept an eye on the weather reports and waited for a period of mild, dry weather. We also found an adequate Raccoon habitat, with a good fresh-water source, a safe distance from human settlements and roads. When the weather obliged, we set about getting the six Raccoons into carriers. But what goes around comes around. We'd spent weeks teaching them to be wary of humans and now we had to catch them. It was challenging—and fun.

I entered the enclosure with catch pole in hand, and the Raccoons scattered. They seemed immune to the forces of gravity as they ran up the sides of the enclosure and scampered upside down across the ceiling. I gripped my catch pole and waited for my moment.

A catch pole is merely a long pole with a cable that runs through the handle to form an adjustable loop at the end. To capture a Raccoon you have to get the loop over the head and one front leg of the animal, then pull the noose tight. If you only get it over the head and around the neck, you'll choke the animal. If you get it over the head and both legs, the Raccoons slide out.

It took me more than an hour to catch all six Raccoons, and I was only scratched, bitten, and peed on once by each of them. Not a bad average. I was quick to shove them into their separate airline kennels before they could scurry loose again.

At the chosen release site, we opened the kennel doors and the six attic orphans charged out of the crates like Thoroughbreds at the bell. They scattered in all directions, each one climbing the first tree it came to. In their protected enclosure this gang never climbed higher than seven feet, but now they climbed as if their lives depended on it—exactly as they should have. We'd taught them well.

When a couple of them hit the 100-foot mark and it seemed they were going to keep climbing as long as we waited below, we turned and left our bandit-faced charges clinging to their trees.

COLUMBIA BLACKTAIL HIT BY A CAR

It was three a.m. when the phone rang. I'd been asleep for less than an hour since completing a two o'clock seal feeding. In the deep darkness created by the woods in which I live, I fumbled for the telephone. "God I hope it's a wrong number!"

A mechanical sounding voice repeats, "This is Betty at the Sheriff's department."

"Okay Betty, where is it?" I slipped back into the clothes piled on my floor and started down the path through the trees. "I smell like a seal," I thought to myself as I sniffed the sleeve of my sweatshirt.

I stopped by the treatment centre long enough to toss a litre bag of intravenous fluids into a pail of hot water. It would be body temperature when I got back. My '65 Ford pickup carried me into the night. As I rounded the corner just south of the airport entrance, I could see the flashing lights at either end of the street. There were three squad cars, and a small town version of a traffic jam was beginning to accrue. Everyone had been waiting for me to get out of bed. The burning road flares, the spinning red lights, and the alien sounds over the police radios made for a bizarre scene. I felt as if I was driving back into the dream I left fifteen minutes before. Added to that, staggering toward me down the centre yellow line came a Columbia Black-Tailed Deer, wrapped in a strange aura from the lights behind. When he limped into the glare of a spotlight, I saw his eyes clearly. He was more dazed than I was.

I estimated his weight to be about 140 pounds, then went back to the truck to prepare a couple of sedative darts. I once used a CO_2 dart pistol to sedate, but the darts hit the animal with too much impact. They also explode with a bang and produce a flash of light, neither of which helps to calm the animal. Now I'm proficient with a blow tube and lightweight hypodermic darts. It causes much less stress to the animal and saves me the anxiety of pointing a gun.

My hands weren't very steady this particular morning, so I crouched down and rested an elbow on my knee. One deep inhale, then a sharp exhale through tightly pursed lips, and the dart was on target. The Buck didn't even flinch. What he did was turn toward the

woods on the side of the road and head for cover. Usually a Deer in trouble will head for as much cover as it can find. Losing the sedated Deer in the woods would pretty much spoil my plans for him, so I followed closely. I inserted a second dart into the tube and, as the

stupefied Buck paused about ten yards in front of me, hit him again. Down he crashed as if I had pulled his legs out from under him. A police officer and I rolled him over onto a blanket. I shook my head in resignation. Both my darts were crushed. It's the buttered toast principle. They always fall on the side with the darts. With the officer's help, I loaded the Deer onto the truck bed.

It was four a.m. by the time I got back to the Centre, time to see about pulling this guy through his crisis. I parked under the spotlights next to the treatment room and started to work on him in the back of

the truck. I shaved a patch of fur from his neck, felt for his jugular vein, then inserted the needle to ease a steady drip of warmed fluids into his body. This helps counter shock. I also administered homeopathic remedies: Arnica (Leopard's Bane) to reduce swelling, ease pain, and seal off leaking blood vessels, and Aconite (Monkshood). Aconite works to calm an animal's fear or anxiety. And while it's valuable in treating inflammations and fevers, its ability to quell the fear-of-death syndrome is what makes it so beneficial for wild animals suddenly in the hands of a predator: humans.

Our success rate for saving Deer hit by automobiles is low. Even when their injuries aren't life threatening, Deer will too often start to wake up from sedation, realize they are captive among predators, and die. It's both frustrating and disheartening.

While the Deer slept, I did a basic examination. His gums and

mucus membranes were deathly pale, typical of shock, but I didn't feel any broken bones or see outward signs of serious soft tissue damage. Although his respiration was shallow and rapid, his lungs sounded clear. As the last of the second litre of fluids drained into his bloodstream, I prepared to drive him back to a holding pen where I was determined he would recuperate.

In the morning I found the Buck hiding in the weeds in the corner of the pen, just where I deposited him the night before. He appeared to be alert and watched me with great distrust as I left food and fresh water on the opposite side of the pen. Afraid my presence

would incite him to make a blind run at the fence, I kept my distance. He kept his head low to the ground as if there was a chance I hadn't noticed him. He reminded me of a child that puts his hands over his eyes and says, "You can't see me."

This particular deer pen was separate from the ones used for the orphaned fawns. It was roughly fifty feet long and fifty feet wide, with an eight-foot fence on three sides and a five-foot fence on the fourth side. The fourth side was built high enough to contain an injured Deer, but low enough that once feeling better, the animal could hurdle it easily. The weeds in the pen were waist deep, offering the animals cover and, hopefully, some feeling of safety and well being. Stress can build in a captive wild animal, compromising the immune system until the animal slowly slips away. Keeping the animals as calm and isolated as possible is a must.

I left the Buck alfalfa, apples, and some fresh leafy branches, called browse, planning to return at the end of the day. As the hours passed, I kept thinking about the wounded Black-Tail, worried I might have missed something during my examination. But I resisted the urge to look in on him, knowing he needed his space. As the afternoon turned to evening, I completed my rounds of all the animals. It's a good idea to look in on every animal before the sun goes down. I look into their eyes if possible. This can tell me a lot. I check the condition of their fur or feathers. Do they look lethargic, have they eaten, do their feces look normal? The night can be very long for an animal turning critical.

When my rounds were done, I went to check on the Buck. I entered the deer pen from the far corner where I'd left the food. The flake of alfalfa had been scattered about. The apples were gone and the browse looked like a tree in winter. All good signs. I approached the resting Deer, and he tried to press himself into the earth in an attempt to disappear. His left eye looked foggy, so, quietly and slowly, I moved closer, then closer yet. The Buck lay dead still. I still couldn't get a good look at the bad eye, so I reached out to move his chin slightly. The touch of my hand on his face made him explode to his feet while simultaneously kicking me hard into the fence.

This burst of adrenaline that brought him in an instant to his full height also sent him racing across the pen towards the eight-foot wall. I watched awestruck as he bounded through the high weeds and with one powerful, neck-stretching leap, launched himself towards the sky showing over the top of the barrier. I would have staked my life that he couldn't clear that fence.

Unfortunately, I was right. He fell short of the mark, with his antlers connecting with the wire squares in the top two feet of the fence. Not only had he failed his escape, but he also managed to hang himself by his antlers from the top of the fence. His body slammed against the wooden barrier as his legs flailed in all directions. He continuously bellowed out sounds I had never heard from a Deer.

It took me a moment to react to this new crisis. I ran to his aid but could not get near him because of his sharp hooves flying in all directions. I ran across the pen, out the gate, and around to the back side. All I could see were the points of his antlers protruding through the wire squares above my head.

I needed wire cutters and I needed them now! I began the heart-pounding sprint back to the Centre. As I ran, I could hear his hooves clawing and scraping against the wood, and that bellowing. Sometimes I hear it still. Pushing volunteers aside as I threw open doors, I found the necessary tool. Outside, I commandeered the closest vehicle and bounced back across the rutted field, my head banging on the cab's ceiling. I was back at the pen in seconds.

The Deer hung limply against the wall. A few snips with the wire cutters and the Buck collapsed to the ground. To my surprise, he seemed no worse for the ordeal. He stood up and walked steadily back to his side of the pen and lay back down in the weeds. I watched through the fence for a few minutes and then went home. I felt pretty fortunate that my good intentions hadn't killed him.

The next morning my first stop was the deer pen. I approached the gate with newly inspired caution. I didn't see any sign of the Buck as I scanned the pen. He was successfully concealing himself from me. Slowly, I walked back and forth through the weeds. I have to admit, I never expected what I found. He was gone. All that remained was a small tuft of fur caught in a wire on the top edge of the low fence. That little tuft of fur moving gently in the wind told his whole story.

About the Island Wildlife Natural Care Centre

There are no signs to point the way, but the entrance is easy enough to find: the drive turns away from St. Mary's Lake and winds up through conifers and spindly arbutus trees to the Island Wildlife Natural Care Centre. Once a private residence over-looking Trincomali Channel, the cedar-shake dwelling now serves as an office, surgery and recovery area for injured wildlife. A lustrous parquet floor lends the place a sumptuous air, as if this could be the Mayo Clinic of wildlife refuges, a sanctuary where only the best treatment will do.

Truth be told, that's the way Jeff Lederman likes to think about it.

"I'll do whatever it takes to cure an animal," he says with conviction. "Whatever's least invasive." Therapeutic treatments are the Centre's forte—homeopathy, herbal therapy, reiki, and physical therapy, to name a few. But they're not the only remedies available.

"I'm not hardline about it," Jeff continues. "An animal deeply in the throes of infection needs a drug... Everything hinges on what's best for the animal."

Adjacent to the surgery room, a garage has been converted to serve as a food preparation area for the Centre's charges. An addition has been built onto one end and at first glance the roofed enclosure appears to be some kind of spa, with its platoon of bathtubs neatly in rows. It turns out that this is the intensive care unit for injured harbour seals—Jeff's specialty, the reason he is here in the first place. Several circular pools lie just outside, swimming tanks for seals on the mend. The lucky ones. The survival stories.

Elsewhere on the four-acre property there is an aviary, a deer pen, and several mews for raptors in recovery. A flight cage is planned, as are special enclosures for recovering seabirds and injured raccoons. All this conversion and construction in a few short months and there's still a mountain of projects to complete and problems that require immediate attention.

It takes perseverance to build a Centre like this. Belief in a dream is about the only tool that will cut through all the red tape.

Starting with Canadian Immigration. Here's an American citizen who wants to move to Saltspring Island to start a non-profit venture. 'Never heard of such a breed!' comes the official Canadian response. 'Why not stay at home and care for U.S. wildlife?'

Answer: 'Animals know no boundaries; wildlife migrates.' Eventually, Jeff is granted a two-year residence permit to see if his ideas will fly.

More permit wrangling ensues - an alphabet soup of federal and provincial regulations to untangle. Environment Canada is in charge of migratory birds, the provincial Ministry of Environment has the say on almost all other wildlife. Except marine mammals—the

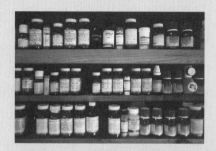

Department of Fisheries and Oceans presides over them. Gradually, all this paperwork hatches one of the few wildlife centres in B.C. permitted to care for all indigenous species.

Still another legal hurdle has to be cleared to register the Centre as a non-profit society. Amid all the fine print, Jeff remains determined to keep things simple. The society's Board of Directors consists of three people, only two of whom can vote: Jeff and one other. "It's a kind of dictatorship," he admits, "but I've seen fatal mistakes happen elsewhere and after all the hard work I'm not going to let that happen here."

For technical assistance, the Centre relies on an advisory board. Support from a local vet is a prerequisite for the environment ministry permit. Other advisors include two marine biologists, a homeopathic doctor, and a vet who specializes in alternative therapies. Based both locally and farther afield, these specialists are only an e-mail request away from contributing their insights to unusual cases, advising on treatments, or assisting on site when needed.

Land, buildings, permits, boards—they're the Centre's flesh and blood. In order to succeed, though, non-profit ventures like this depend on a sturdy

back-bone of volunteers. Recruiting and training people to work with wild animals is naturally an ongoing task.

As is fundraising. Jeff has several creative ideas simmering on the back-burner. "Too many centres are always begging the local community for help," he says. "That is not our attitude. We want to be self-sustaining." Developing a line of herbal treatments for commercial use, publishing an informative quarterly newsletter for society members, publishing more books like this one, setting up a wildlife adoption program, holding art auctions—these are some of the recipes being prepared to keep the Centre afloat.

It all adds up to a 24-hour-on-call, seven-day-a-week undertaking. "It's not glamorous, especially when an animal dies," says Jeff.

To survive, the Centre itself needs close tending from some full-time, paid staff. Even with all his energy and enthusiasm, Jeff is first to admit that his own resources are finite. "But it just takes one or two incredible patrons to turn things around," he adds philosophically. "People don't invest in dreams. They invest in what's already there."

Charles Hart - September 1997

ABOUT THE AUTHOR

Over his 45 years, Jeff Lederman has traveled a winding road. Born into a suburban Chicago middle-class family, Jeff rejected a career in law in favour of the world of art. Over time, Jeff's large-scale abstract paintings, contemporary furniture designs, and sculpture made their way into galleries and private collections across the country.

In the late 80s, Jeff moved to Santa Fe, New Mexico. There, through exposure to his first wildlife rehabilitation centre, his interest in art was engulfed by new discovery and a sudden awareness of a world he had never known and an ecosystem he would soon embrace. A spontaneous passion to nurture and protect wildlife has dictated his life's priorities ever since.

Applying natural medications and homeopathic techniques that had long been a part of his personal regimen, Jeff has evolved into one of the most knowledgeable naturopathic caregivers in the field of wildlife rehabilitation. He is consulted regularly via his website (http://www.island-net.com/~wildlife) by other rehab facilities worldwide.

In the spring of 1997 he founded the Island Wildlife Natural Care Centre on Saltspring Island, B.C. *Cries of the Wild* is Jeff's first book and serves to commemorate the creation of the new wildlife centre and help make us aware of the daily challenges faced by those who work to save wildlife. All author royalties are being donated to the Centre.

PHOTO CREDITS

Scott Terrell-
*Skagit Valley
Herald*, front
cover photo
Lill Hale
pages 38, 82

Valerie Wells
page 15
Linda Wells
page 135
Charles Hart
pages 141 to 143

Kelley Balcomb
back-cover Orca
and page 12
C. Fortuna, Tethys
Research Institute
page 68

Stefania Gaspari
pages 74, 75, 76
and author photo
page 144